PADST
LIFEBOATS

AN ILLUSTRATED HISTORY

Nicholas Leach
FOXGLOVE PUBLISHING

To Edward

First published 2012, second edition 2018

ISBN 9781909540132

Published by
Foxglove Publishing Ltd
Lichfield
United Kingdom
Tel 07940 905046

© Nicholas Leach 2018

Typesetting and origination by
Nicholas Leach/Foxglove Publishing

Printed by Hobbs the Printers Ltd,
Totton, Hampshire, SO40 3WX

Contents

Padstow lifeboat 16m
Tamar Spirit of Padstow.
(Nicholas Leach)

Introduction

Padstow lifeboat station, situated on the north Cornish coast, is one of the most famous in the country wth a long and illustrious history. Today the volunteer crew operate a modern twenty-five-knot 16m Tamar class lifeboat from a state-of-the-art lifeboat house at Trevose Head, a picturesque headland overlooking Mother Ivey's Bay and out across the Atlantic, which has been used since the 1960s after the station moved from its original location at Hawker's Cove, where lifeboats had been operated since the 1820s. The Cove is a few miles north of Padstow town, which itself was built around a small harbour and was once a busy port. The Pool of Padstow was once thronged with coastal traders in the days of sail. Nowadays, the harbour divides its facilities between the local and visiting fishing fleet, and a thriving leisure trade focussed on visitors and the tourist trade has developed.

The Doom Bar and Hell Bay at the mouth of the Camel Estuary have always been a great danger to shipping, and numerous craft have been wrecked there after being caught in westerly gales. Nearly 300 vessels have been lost or stranded, many sailors have drowned, and three lifeboats have been lost in less than a square mile of the wave-pounded sands. As early as 18 December 1753 the wine-laden sloop *Joseph Ange*, of Treguier, was wrecked at Porthmizzen, with her crew lucky to survive. Another eighteenth-century shipwreck in the area occurred at Harlyn Bay on 5 January 1792, when the vessel *Caroline*, of and for Chepstow from London, drove on to the wide flat beach.

The three lifeboats were lost in two tragedies. The first was in February 1867, when five of the lifeboat crew were drowned after the lifeboat capsized, and the second in April 1900 after the ketch *Peace and Plenty* was wrecked on rocks. In going to the ketch's aid, the pulling lifeboat *Arab* was struck by a tremendous sea which buried the lifeboat, washed eight of her crew overboard and broke all her oars. The lifeboat was wrecked on the rocks, but the crew got ashore safely. The steam lifeboat *James Stevens No.4*, going to the same casualty, was caught by a heavy swell and capsized. Eight of her crew of eleven were drowned.

These two events helped to shape the future development of the station, particularly the latter incident, which resulted in the RNLI building and operating a steam tug at Padstow, which worked with a large sailing lifeboat, to provide a unique set-up that was never repeated. The station thus had a steam lifeboat, one of only six to be built by the RNLI; a steam tug, of which only one was built; and has also operated early examples of several different classes of lifeboat, including one of only four 60-61ft Barnetts, the first lifeboat with twin screws and twin engines; the second 48ft 6in Oakley self-righter; the third 47ft Tyne; and the fourth 16m Tamar to be built. The station has thus been at the forefront of RNLI lifeboat design during the twentieth century. And, today, the 2006-built boathouse provides the volunteer lifeboat crew with all the facilities needed to provide an effective and efficient modern rescue service.

Acknowledgements

This book could not have been written without the support, help and enthusiasm of Mike England, the station's full-time mechanic. His hospitality during my visits to the station and eagerness to find information and photographs for inclusion have ensured that this book is as complete and up-to-date as possible. He is a true lifeboat enthusiast and I am extremely grateful to him. for all his help Thanks also to rest of the Padstow volunteer lifeboat crew for their cooperation. Trevor Sharpe's research into the station's history proved useful, as did the previous books about the station by Claude Berry and Grahame Farr. At the RNLI, I am grateful to Nathan Williams for providing images for possible inclusion, and to Hayley Whiting and Joanna Bellis of the Heritage Trust for facilitating my research at the RNLI library in Poole. Thanks also to Peter Edey, Tony Denton, Tim Stevens, Paul Richards, Iain Booth and John Harrop for supplying images for possible inclusion.

Nicholas Leach
Lichfield, July 2018

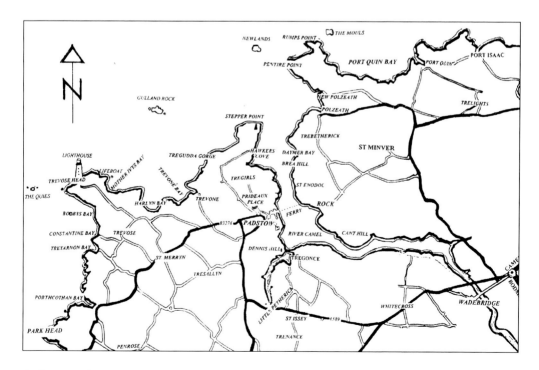

The First Lifeboats

Before a national body responsible for life-saving at sea had been founded, local individuals and organisations provided the impetus as well as the funds and management necessary for a lifeboat. Lifeboats were established at those places where vessels were most frequently at risk, such as Penzance on Cornwall's south coast, and where a crew could readily be obtained. This was often at or relatively close to a port, such as Padstow, where a natural harbour was formed by the estuary of the river Camel. This had been used by shipping from the earliest times, and was a prosperous port with a vibrant commercial seaborne trade. The Pool of Padstow was regularly filled by brigs, brigantines, schooners and smacks, and often visited by the square riggers in the timber and emigrant trades. However, the Camel estuary had a treacherous entrance, which caused difficulty even for those who were familiar with it, and it proved to be the last resting place of many ships. Many vessels were lost here, where the aptly named Doom Bar and Hell Bay caught vessels out while they were running in before the westerly gales, usually just when their exhausted crews thought they had found shelter. Even those with local knowledge often found the winds under Stepper Point could send them out of the narrow shore-hugging deep water channel.

Although the dangers of the harbour suggested a lifeboat was needed at the port, before a rescue boat was provided, rescues were undertaken by local boats. Two early rescues, which feature in the records of the Royal National Institution for the Preservation of Life from Shipwreck (RNIPLS, forerunner of the RNLI), were probably both completed using local gigs. The first was in early 1825, when eight were saved from the snow *New Braganza* of London, a Lisbon packet, by William Hibley and four other Padstow men. The second was in November 1826 when seven men were saved from the brig *Lord Dupplin*, of London, which was caught out in a gale and driven onto the Dunbar Sands. A pilot boat put off to her assistance, but was caught in the heavy breaking seas and capsized, and three of the pilots were drowned. Another pilot boat put out to help and managed to save ten men and a boy from the brig, which soon afterwards broke up.

With the dangers of the estuary so evident, moves were made to provide a lifeboat in the mid-1820s. A collection among the local merchants and townspeople, to which the RNIPLS made a contribution of £10, provided the funds and Tredwen, a local boatbuilder, constructed the craft at a cost of £50. She was completed in 1827, was 23ft in length and pulled by four oars. A contemporary description of her stated: 'she has both ends alike so as to row out against a sea and return without turning her, thus avoiding the risk of being upset.' She was supposedly named *Mariner's Friend*, and was kept at first on the Quay. Under whose auspices it was managed initially is not clear, but two years later the Padstow Harbour Association for the Preservation of Life and Property from Shipwreck was founded and took over the boat. This Association, unique in Cornwall, was established at a public meeting on 11 November 1829, with the intention to work towards 'the preservation of life and property from shipwreck, by rendering more effectual assistance to vessels entering the Harbour of Padstow in tempestuous weather'. One of the aims of the new organisation was 'to provide accommodation for the lifeboat and Manby's Mortar Apparatus' that were already in operation, and the lifeboat thus came under their authority.

The Association was founded under the patronage of the Reverend Charles Prideaux-Brune, with John Paynter and the Rev W. Rawlings acting as trustees. The first subscription list included a £100 contribution from Lloyd's, as well as sums from many of the gentry, merchants and shipmasters in the Duchy, the Merchant Venturers' Society of Bristol, and Messrs Vivian and Sons, a Swansea company. The Association had far-sighted plans to reduce the hazards of the harbour. In the first two years they had three large capstans placed on the inner side of Stepper Point, two buoys moored in the channel, and the 40ft daymark built, which can still be seen on the highest part of the headland. Other works included the building of houses for pilots, sheds for hawsers, and the Manby mortar apparatus, with connecting roads, landing places and slipways.

The 40ft daymark at Stepper Point was erected in the 1820s by the Padstow Harbour Association. (Grahame Farr)

The lifeboat was moved to Hawker's Cove, a small sheltered inlet nearer the mouth of the estuary from where it could be launched more easily. A lifeboat house was built there by the Association, possibly in 1829, and this remains standing, now with living accommodation above. While commercial trading concerns could see the benefit of a lifeboat to their own operations, at a general meeting of the association on 25 June 1831, the Rev Francis John Hext, Rector of Melland, gave £25 'in acknowledgement of the gallant and successful exertions of the Padstow boatmen, about nineteen years since, in assisting to bring an Admiralty Tender within Stepper Point; and

towards the further persecution of the works thereon'. Other subscribers included individuals from as far afield as Plymouth, London and Fowey, as well as businesses from Hayle and Llandore.

The first Annual General Meeting of the Association was held a couple of weeks later, on 6 July 1831, at which the Chairman, H. P. Rawlings, reported that they had 'preserved six vessels from total wreck' (sic). These vessels were listed as follows: on 21 November 1830, the sloop *Thomas* of Falmouth, the sloop *Mary Ann and Eliza* of London, and the schooner *Pomona* of Padstow had all been saved. In 1831 three vessels had been saved: on 1 February the schooner *Stephen Knight* of Plymouth, and on 5 February the brigs *Speculator* of Exeter and *Violet* of Arundel. Details of how these vessels were saved are not recorded, while a list of expenditure did not mention the lifeboat and the majority of the money was spent on capstans and capstan houses.

At the Association's second Annual General Meeting in July 1832 it was announced that 'a substantial six-oared boat, well calculated for a heavy sea' had been obtained at a cost of £20 11s, and this was kept at Stepper Point, 'where she is available at the shortest notice'. This vessel, probably a heavy gig in form, was intended to be used for taking out hawsers and other hobbling work, but was also used for life-saving duties. She was usually permanently manned, something that probably accounts for the almost total lack of rescues by the Tredwen-built lifeboat. In fact the only known rescue by the lifeboat was the result of the Associations boat being disabled. An account of this rescue appears in the minutes of the National Lifeboat Institution, which contain the following entry:

'Read letter from Mr Kent, Padstow, of 2 December (1833), stating that the brig *Albion* (Hudson) from Youghall to London, ran on the Dunbar (sic) Sands on 29 November in a most violent gale with a heavy ground sea. The Harbour

The small harbour at Padstow was once busy with coastal shipping, but is now largely a tourist attraction for visitors to Cornwall. In this image from the early twentieth century, the town's pulling and sailing lifeboats can be seen to the left.

Boat belonging to the Association manned with volunteers was upset going to her assistance – as the Custom House boat also received damage – after which Mr Giles, a Master of a vessel, and seven seamen volunteered their services in the lifeboat and proceeded to the vessel, took four men of her crew (out of five) on board and continued alongside, spending about half an hour endeavouring to prevail on the Master to get into the boat; at that time the line fastening the boat parted and the Master was by that means left on board the vessel. The vessel soon after fell over and afterwards sunk . . . Ordered: That the Silver medal be presented to Mr Giles and eight sovereigns award to be distributed to him and the other seven men.'

As well as being the body responsible for funding, organising and maintaining lifeboats and lifeboat stations, it was also the practice of the RNIPLS to award 'medallions or pecuniary rewards . . . to those who rescue lives in cases of shipwreck', and several rescues off Padstow received the nascent Institution's recognition with Mr Giles being the first to be so rewarded. The next incident was on the morning of 30 November 1836 when the Association's boat made an outstanding rescue during a severe north-westerly gale after the smack *Britannia*, of Jersey, and the schooner *Jane*, of Swansea, ran for the harbour on the ebb tide. The smack had lost her mainsail, mainboom, foretopsail and boat, and she was taking in water. When the two vessels reached the shelter of Stepper Point, both were caught in the cross winds under the cliffs and, to the horror of the onlookers, collided with each other and, locked together, drifted on to the Doom Bar. Messervey, the master of the smack, leapt on board the schooner, but at that moment she hit the bottom and the two vessels parted, and the smack was driven further ashore with three men still on board.

The mortar and rockets were quickly brought from their shed, readied and fired, but in spite of the favourable wind the lines fell short of their target, and the schooner began to break up, with the six or seven men on board being thrown into the sea and drowned. A boat was the only way the remaining men clinging to the smack's rigging could be saved, and so the Association's boat at Stepper Point was launched, as the *Royal Cornwall Gazette* reported: 'the Harbour Association's boat was dispatched to the smack, and happily, the remaining three men were removed from their perilous situation, and brought safe to the shore.' The bare facts do scant justice to a feat of great heroism and Captain Mitchell Brown Wade, of the Padstow brig *Dew Drop*, who took the steering oar of the boat, was awarded the Silver medal by the RNIPLS, while his helpers received monetary awards. Captain Wade also collected clothing for the rescued and money to pay for the journey to their homes.

In 1841 a Silver medal was awarded to Joseph Mortley, Chief Officer, HM Coastguard, for his gallant services to the brig *Britannia*, carrying coal on passage from Cardiff, which was driven onto the Doom Bar in heavy seas on 31 March. Only the tops of the brig's rigging could be seen by the time the rescue was being effected, so Mortley and his men set up the Dennett's rocket apparatus and managed to get a line aboard the casualty at the first attempt. The master, mate and four seamen were saved by the apparatus, with the rescue being completed

by the Coastguardsmen going out onto the rocks and having the heavy seas breaking over both them and those they had rescued.

In 1843 Richard Tredwen, a member of the shipbuilding family, led a boat's crew to rescue seven from the brig *Towan*, of Cork, on 28 October. The brig went aground on the Doom Bar and, after her boat was stove in, no pilot would put out to help so Tredwen and seven others manned a boat brought from the town and took out ropes to the brig. He then boarded and saved the vessel, as well as her crew. For this gallant rescue, Tredwen too was awarded the RNIPLS Silver Medal. He may have used the lifeboat, or perhaps it was a boat from his yard for all the shipbuilders had a gig, manned by apprentices, so that they could race to the river mouth to be first on board incoming vessels, particularly disabled ones, and contract for repair work. Tredwen was a man of great bravery and, two years later, he distinguished himself again when the snow *William Pitt*, of Sunderland, was wrecked and he ran into the breaking surf to save James Hewson, the sole survivor of a crew of eleven. She was bound from Alexandria for Gloucester, and ran on the Doom Bar. Tredwen's gig and crew made a further brave rescue in January 1854, when the schooner *Sarah*, after straining at her anchors for six hours on the very edge of the Doom Bar, parted her cables and became a total wreck, her crew being picked up from their own boat.

The other Silver medal-winning rescue to take place during the first half of the nineteenth century was undertaken on 8 December 1847 after the vessel *Marchioness of Abercorn*, on passage from Quebec to London, was wrecked near Padstow. Captains William Johns, William Dark and William Found launched a small boat, and pulled through very heavy seas to reach the wreck, from which they brought a line ashore. Four survivors were brought to safety using a small

A model of Mariner's Friend, the first lifeboat at Padstow. (By courtesy of RNLI)

The original lifeboat house (to the left) used by the Harbour Association lifeboat, with the house (in the centre of the photo) built by the RNLI in 1864, after it had taken over the station, for the first Albert Edward lifeboat. (Grahame Farr, by courtesy of the RNLI)

boat, but this capsized during the second trip and two men were tragically drowned. Finally, using a hawser, the remainder of the crew, consisting of the master and twenty men, were brought ashore. The three Captains were each awarded the Silver medal for their part in this rescue.

Throughout this period, the Tredwen-built lifeboat of 1827 remained on station, but seems remained unused. The 1843 Select Committee on Shipwrecks, which published a list of lifeboats around the coast, included the boat at Padstow, describing it as being maintained at the expense of the 'Shipwreck Institution', and under the charge of the 'officer commanding the station'. The principal dimensions of the boat were given as 22ft in length, 6ft 4in in breadth, and with a depth of 2ft 6in, pulling four oars, but the Report says nothing about its condition. The *Northumberland Report* on the state of the country's lifesaving services, published in 1851, did comment on the boat, describing it as being 'in fair repair', although the dimensions listed differed from those provided in 1843, with the boat measuring 23ft by 6ft 6in by2ft 6in. The 1851 Report also stated that there were nine rockets and four mortars at the station, with the rockets having been used to save six lives. However, despite the *Northumberland Report's* description of the boat, in June 1855 it was said to have been condemned, and in the following month John Dyer Bryant, the Receiver of Admiralty Droits at Padstow, wrote to the newly-reformed Royal National Lifeboat Institution (RNLI) to ask if they would be prepared to send a new one. The importance of the station was beyond question and prompt action was taken, with the RNLI bringing the station under its auspices.

RNLI Pulling Lifeboats

B y the time the Royal National Lifeboat Institution (RNLI) took over at Padstow, it had been in existence for more than half a century. Founded in March 1824 at a meeting in London as the Royal National Institution for the Preservation of Life from Shipwreck, it was responsible for 'the preservation of lives and property from shipwreck.' This encompassed the funding, building, operation, maintenance and organisation of lifeboats and lifeboat stations. Initially quite successful, the new organisation added to the number of lifeboats in operation but, by the 1840s, the organisation's efforts started to falter through lack of funds. The Institution found raising money for lifeboats difficult and enjoyed only limited success in providing a nationwide lifeboat service. Its annual income dwindled during the 1830s and 1840s until, by 1850, with no public appeals made for over a decade, financed were at their lowest. Improvements were essential if life-saving work around the coasts was to continue and these started on 2 May 1851 with the appointment of Algernon, Duke of Northumberland as President. Through his energy and efforts during the 1850s, working alongside the newly-appointed secretary Richard Lewis, much-needed improvements to the Institution were implemented.

During the 1850s the organisation was renamed the Royal National Lifeboat Institution to more accurately reflect its aims and objectives, and it began to absorb the local life-saving organisations that had sprung up in the preceding half century or so. This included Padstow where the lifeboat, by July 1855, was reported by Captain Davies to be inefficient and, 'though lately patched up, nothing can be made of her'. Steps were therefore taken to improve matters. On 29 October 1855 the Harbour Trust promised to provide £10 per annum towards a new lifeboat and at a meeting on 6 December 1855 the RNLI Committee decided that a lifeboat measuring 30ft by 6ft should be built for the station, based on the design of James Peake, Assistant Master Shipwright in HM Dockyard. The Peake-designed self-righting

The notice calling for a meeting to as the RNLI to establish a branch in Padstow, dated 3 December 1855.

Port of Padstow.

Life Boat.

The Subscribers to the Funds of the Padstow Branch of the Royal National Life Boat Institution, and all who feel interested in the establishment of a Life Boat at this Port, are requsted to meet in the Public Rooms Padstow, on Saturday, the 22nd day of December instant at noon.

C. G. Prideaux Brune,
Chairman of the Committee.

Padstow, 3rd December, 1855.

lifeboat was the standard type of the period and the boat for Padstow was built by Forrestt at Limehouse, in London, who were the RNLI's usual boatbuilder.

To fund the boat, the local committee, formed under the chairmanship of C.G. Prideaux Brune with the Rev Richard Tyacke as Secretary, collected £160, of which the Duke of Cornwall contributed £25 and also gave permission for the boat to be named *Albert Edward*. The new boat was completed by her builder on 2 April 1856 and on 28 May 1856 was sent to Penzance by steamship before being towed to Padstow by Revenue Cruiser. The local committee reported the arrival of the new boat on 3 June 1856 at which point she was taken to the boathouse at Hawker's Cove. When the RNLI took over the station, it continued operating from Hawker's Cove in the original boathouse. However, in 1863 a new boathouse was built by the RNLI alongside the Harbour Association house. On 28 July 1856 Captain Ward, the RNLI Inspector, and the committee recommended two carriages and in October 1856 plans were drawn up for a carriage house to be built on the east side of the harbour to speed up launching.

The new lifeboat performed her first service on 14 March 1857 when, in a heavy north-westerly gale, the schooner *Haberdine* ran for the harbour seeking shelter, but was driven onto the Doom Bar. The lifeboat, crewed by seven men, took off four crew from the schooner shortly before she became a total wreck. It was reported that the boat behaved entirely to the satisfaction of the crew and on several subsequent occasions her manageability in heavy seas was commented upon, a notable occasion being a practice launch when a heavy sea knocked several men from the thwarts. Even though a subsequent sea again buried them, she did not 'broach to.'

Albert Edward's second service came on 8 March 1859 when she went to the brig *Gonsalve*, of Nantes, which was caught in bad weather, unable to weather Trevose and was forced to run for Padstow harbour. As she reached the lee of Stepper Point she was caught in winds and, without sufficient steerage, the tide and heavy seas drove her on the Doom Bar. The lifeboat was launched and, despite being repeatedly filled by the heavy seas, saved the crew of seven, with the brig breaking up soon afterwards. Seven days later the lifeboat undertook a similar service to the schooner *Frederick William*, of Ipswich, when she was launched through a heavy north-westerly gale to save the schooner's four crew and the pilot. The schooner was also saved, and was subsequently repaired at Padstow, being later sold to a Looe owner for further trading. For this and the service a week before Coxswain Daniel Shea, Commissioned Boatman of the Coast Guard, was awarded the Silver medal by the RNLI; for the *Gonsalve* rescue, the Emperor of the French presented a silver medal to each of the crew.

On 22 January 1860 the ship *James Alexander* was wrecked off Padstow during a very heavy gale. Coxswain Daniel Shea, at about 8am the following day, assembled a crew, having spotted the vessel trying to weather Trevose Head and make for the harbour. But the ship failed to get round the headland and went ashore about six miles from Padstow. Led by Coxswain Shea, the lifeboat crew made for the spot where the vessel had foundered, arriving at the scene to see four men jump overboard and attempt to swim ashore. Two of them were totally

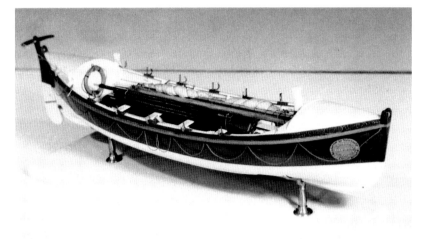

Model of the lifeboat Albert Edward, a 32ft ten-oared self-righter, which was on station from 1864 to 1883, fuded by Captain R. Tyson's City of Bristol fund. This RNLI presentation model was photographed in City Museum, Bristol. (Grahame Farr, by courtesy of RNLI)

exhausted, so James Knight rushed into the sea and helped them safely ashore. In the meantime, the Coastguard, using rockets, got a line aboard the ship. Shea then stripped himself and tried to swim to a rock close to the casualty, shouting to the remainder of the crew to stay with their vessel until the rocket apparatus had been readied, and eventually the crew were saved. For his efforts the Silver Second-Service clasp was awarded to Coxswain Shea.

On 1 January 1861 a vessel was reported on the Doom Bar in a heavy south-westerly gale, and the lifeboat crew, after a hard struggle through the difficult conditions, found the brigantine *Nugget*, of Bideford, which had been driven from her anchors earlier in the night. As she was deserted, and knowing the crew had been aboard the previous evening, the lifeboat crew began a long and difficult search in the dark. Eventually they found the men in their boat riding dangerously at anchor in a hazardous position, unable to row further against the gale. The five men were taken aboard the lifeboat and, as the lifeboat drew clear, the small boat sank under the weight of a particularly heavy sea.

On the night of 8 November 1862 the sloop *Loftus*, of Padstow, in entering her home port, was forced to anchor in Hell Bay, facing a strong westerly wind and heavy seas. At daylight she was seen from the shore flying a flag of distress. *Albert Edward* was launched to her assistance and, rowing through a very heavy sea, the lifeboat crew reached the scene and managed to take off her crew of four. Saving the vessel was not possible, and the sloop shortly afterwards was driven ashore when her anchor chains snapped, quickly breaking up.

The last two services by *Albert Edward* took place on the night of 18 March 1863 in a strong northerly gale and heavy sea. She was launched first to the brigantine *Pandema* of Plymouth, bound from Cardiff for London with railway iron, which had struck the Doom Bar. The lifeboat crew, with great difficulty, saved the brigantine's eight crew. As they were returning to station, they saw the schooner Betsey, of Brixham, bound from South Wales for Plymouth with coals, also strike the Bar. The first crew were immediately landed, and the lifeboat went out again into the gale to rescue a further five men from the second casualty.

The second Albert Edward (1864-1883)

The pulling lifeboat *Albert Edward*, the first lifeboat supplied by the RNLI, gave excellent service at Padstow, saving almost forty lives during her career, but in 1863 the RNLI decided she should be replaced by a slightly more powerful ten-oared boat, which was deemed suitable for the station. Funds to pay for the boat had been raised at Bristol, through the efforts of Captain Robert Tryon, RN, and she was given the same name as her predecessor, *Albert Edward*, after HRH the Prince of Wales. Measuring 32ft by 7ft 4in, she was only slightly larger than her predecessor, but she had four more oars. The boat was taken to Bristol by the Great Western Railway, free of charge, and publicly exhibited there on 15 June 1864, during which she was named and launched on the lake at the Zoological Gardens. She was conveyed to Padstow free of charge via the Bristol and Exeter and South Devon and Cornwall Railway Companies and was ready for service in Cornwall a few days later. A new and larger house was built at Hawker's Cove at a cost of £272 1s 0d, and this was used until 1931, when a motor lifeboat was supplied to Padstow.

The first services by the new lifeboat took place on 26 November 1864, when she was launched three times to help vessels come safely into harbour during a very heavy north-westerly gale. On the first launch her help was not needed, but she later helped the schooner *Elizabeth,* of Llanelli, and the lugger *Marie Estella* of Nantes in separate incidents.

The next service proved to be one of the most notable in the history of the station. On the evening of 29 December 1865 a vessel was seen anchored near Hell Bay in a very strong south-westerly gale flying her ensign signalling she was in distress. *Albert Edward* was launched, and with the favourable wind, soon reached the scene to find the barque *Juliet*, of Greenock, bound for London with rum and sugar, rolling heavily and in difficulty. The lifeboat was anchored and drifted down towards the barque until she was under the casualty's stern, rising and falling with the waves. Seventeen men were on board and, although sped was of the essence if they were to get aboard the lifeboat and to safety, jumping across was very risky. But the crew were soon aboard the lifeboat, and the Captain was snatched off last, with the lifeboat then heading back towards its anchor. Once clear of the wreck, sail was set, and she soon gathered speed.

Although the rescue had been difficult, returning to shore was equally hard as the deep water channel and Hawker's Cove were straight to windward, so little progress was made leaving Coxswain William Hills to consider running out of the harbour before the wind to make for Port Isaac. However, he decided to persevere and, after an exhausting pull, the lifeboat eventually landed the rescued men at the Cove. The master of *Juliet*, Captain Drummond, paid a sincere tribute. 'Had not the lifeboat come to our assistance,' he said, 'all hands must certainly have perished, and I cannot speak in terms too strong to express my sense of the conduct of the boat's crew.' His barque later dragged her anchors and became a total wreck on the rocky shore. Coxswain Hills was awarded the Silver medal by the RNLI for his general services, and particularly for the *Juliet* rescue, while the

The site at Hawker's Cove from where the nineteenth century lifeboats were operated. Little now remains of the original boathouse (on left), and the concrete base, keelway and launchway of the 1864 house built by the RNLI remain. (Nicholas Leach)

veteran ex-Coxswain Daniel Shea, who went with them, was awarded a third service clasp to his medal.

Two years later disaster struck the station. On the morning of 6 February 1867 the schooner *Georgiana*, of Boston, Lincolnshire, bound from Rouen for Cork with a crew of five, got caught in a heavy north-westerly gale against which she had been making little progress. So she set course for Padstow harbour, safely rounded Stepper Point and was in comparatively smooth water when it was realised that there was no pilot on station, and nobody to pay out a checking hawser from the capstan on the cliff. Before anything could be done, the schooner was caught in the strong ebb tide and the eddy winds coming over the Point, making it impossible to remedy the situation with her sails. One anchor was dropped, then another, but neither held and she was driven back towards the open sea until, clear of the shelter of the land, she struck the Doom Bar. She was bumped by the waves closer to the St Minver shore, at which point the alarm was raised and the lifeboat crew hurried to Hawker's Cove.

By the time they arrived Coxswain William Hills had launched the boat, with former Coxswain Daniel Shea helping to make up the crew. Although the tide was with them, because of the wind direction, the lifeboat had to be taken to the wreck under oars, struggling through the confused seas. When the boat was windward of the wreck's starboard quarter, the anchor was dropped and the cable was paid out so that she drifted to a position off the casualty's port quarter, ready to close in on the leeward side using the oars. But the lifeboat could not get near enough, the seas proved too much and four oars broke one. To continue with the rescue attempt would have been impossible, returning with the tide rushing out through the narrows was not an option either. So Coxswain Hills headed across the harbour, intending to land at Polzeath where a sandy beach would at least minimise the danger and damage to boat and crew. Once over the sands and clear of the headland they had the weather behind them, and to slow their speed before the wind, the drogue was streamed aft. The motion of the

Memorial on the wall of Padstow church to the lifeboat crew who lost their lives in the disaster of February 1867. (Nicholas Leach)

IN MEMORY OF

DANIEL SHEA, CHIEF OFFICER OF COASTGUARD, 2ND CLASS.
WILLIAM INTROSS, CHIEF BOATMAN.
THOMAS VARCO, COMMISSIONED BOATMAN.
ANDREW TRUSCOTT, TRINITY PILOT.
MICHAEL CRANNELL, MARINER.

THESE BRAVE MEN PERISHED IN THE "ALBERT EDWARD" LIFEBOAT, WHILE NOBLY ENDEAVOURING TO ASSIST THE CREW OF THE "GEORGIANA" OF BOSTON, LINCOLNSHIRE, AT THE ENTRANCE OF PADSTOW HARBOUR, ON THE 6TH OF FEBRUARY 1867.

"THE LORD HATH HIS WAY IN THE WHIRLWIND AND IN THE STORM."
NAHUM I. 3.

"THE WILL OF THE LORD BE DONE."
ACTS XXI. 14.

boat as she lifted on the waves resulted in a series of jerks, while seas repeatedly filled the boat and more oars were broken. Suddenly the canvas of the drogue split and the boat was flung forward, with her stern caught by a wave, and she was capsized almost end over end. All but two of the crew were flung into the heavy surf, and when she capsized a second time soon afterwards she remained overturned for almost five minutes. She then righted and was washed ashore on the sands without any damage whatsoever.

Horrified spectators on the St Minver shore saw the crew struggling to get ashore, being kept afloat by their cork life-jackets but numb and stunned, and in most cases unable to help themselves so men clambered down Trebetherick cliffs to assist. About twenty minutes after the capsize, the local farmer J. Mably managed to throw a rope to the first survivor. He clung to it despite being totally exhausted by his ordeal and was hauled to safety. Eight more of the lifeboat crew were saved in the same way, some being unable to grasp the rope, and having to be seized by rescuers running into the surf. One of the crew was thrown against the rocks with such violence that his cork life-jacket was torn from him, and he was pulled out to sea by the undertow not to be seen again. Two bodies were later washed ashore, but three of the lifeboat crew were never recovered. Meanwhile, *Georgiana* drifted to the nearby shore, her crew in the rigging. The impact of her going aground threw one of the men on board into the sea and he was drowned. As the ship settled on the rocks, the crew managed to get a baulk of timber on a line ashore, and the line was fastened to a hawser which was drawn out to the ship, enabling the shipwrecked to come ashore. The schooner was broken to pieces on the next evening tide.

Of the lifeboat crew on this service, five were drowned: Daniel Shea, William (or Peter) Intross, Thomas Varcoe, Andrew Truscott and Michael Crennel. The survivors were: Coxswain William Hills, Second Coxswain Samuel French, William Mayland, William Harris, William May, Samuel Bate, William Bennett, and James Brenton. The RNLI gave 200 guineas to the fund which was set up for the relief of the four widows and eight orphans left behind, and eventually the fund's total reached £2,188.

In the aftermath of the disaster, volunteers soon came forward to form a new crew. Confidence remained in *Albert Edward* despite the capsize, so a replacement was never considered, and on 8 December 1867 she was launched again. This time she went to the sloop *Telegraph*, of Padstow, which had gone aground on the Doom Bar in a northerly gale with heavy squalls. In approaching the casualty, the lifeboat was driven back by the tide and heavy seas, but the crew persevered and eventually anchored the lifeboat, then dropped down towards the sloop. A rope was secured to the casualty but broke almost at once, so another was thrown and remained fast. The lifeboat was hauled as close as possible to the sloop from which the three men on board were quickly rescued. Course was then set for Hawker's Cove, but in the heavy seas the return journey was particularly hazardous and at one point a heavy sea down the starboard side washed all five oars out of the hands of the crew. Fortunately the rope lanyards secured the oars and they were retrieved enabling the lifeboat to return to station without further incident. Coxswain Hills commented in his report; 'The boat behaved very well, and the crew with perfect discipline and coolness'. The crew men must have had the tragedy ten months before in their thoughts as they battled with the seas, so their efforts and skill are particularly commendable on this occasion.

The next service was on 22 August when the French smack *Jules Josephine*, of Reyneville, was wrecked on the Doom Bar Sands in a heavy south-westerly gale, with *Albert Edward* saving the crew of four. She went out again on 24 October 1868 in a north-westerly gale to the steamer *Augusta*, of Bristol, which had also gone aground on the Doom Bar. The lifeboat crew assisted to save the crew of six after a line had got aboard the casualty from the shore using the Rocket Apparatus. Hawsers from two capstans were used, and although these parted several times, with the assistance of the lifeboat and other means, they were quickly connected again. The steamer was refloated and taken up to the quay in safety, without having sustained much damage.

On 15 January 1869 the lifeboat performed a fine double rescue, in north-westerly gale force winds and very heavy seas. She first launched to the brigantine *Thomas*, of Poole, which was in danger near Stepper Point. While the lifeboat crew were pulling hard towards the scene, eight men from a gig boarded *Thomas* to try to save the vessel, but their boat capsized alongside and was washed away leaving them stranded on the casualty. So the lifeboat took all fourteen men who were on the brigantine, which was subsequently wrecked on the Doom Bar, and then returned to station. Almost as soon as the survivors had been landed than the lifeboat was needed again as the French schooner *Alexandrine*, of Pornic, had gone ashore on the same sandbank, and became a total wreck. The lifeboat put out, but before they had gone far a floating rope from the shore got entangled in the lifeboat's rudder. Crewmember William Corkhill immediately jumped over the stern with a knife and, hanging onto the lifeline with the other hand, cleared the rope. The lifeboatmen were then able

A view over Hawker's Cove looking towards the Camel Estuary in the 1960s, with the original boathouses to the left, and on the right, to the south of the Cove itself, the 1930s boathouse. (Grahame Farr, by courtesy of RNLI)

to save the schooner's six crew, but only just in time, for soon after they had got them safely aboard the lifeboat a huge wave broke over the vessel.

Coxswain Hills' report summed up the rescue in a rather matter-of-fact way: 'I proceeded to the vessel, shipping one or two heavy seas, and lost two oars, got the boat in position, let go the anchor, veered under the lee, took her crew, six in number, on board, and landed them safe at the station'. The Inspecting Officer of Coast Guard, who was an eye-witness of these services, reported that 'the lifeboat was managed most admirably, and that the greatest credit was due to the coxswain and the whole of the boat's crew'.

Another outstanding rescue was undertaken on 2 April 1872, and it was unusual in that it took place in Harlyn Bay, the first time that the lifeboat had been launched from there on her carriage on service. In a strong north-westerly gale and a tremendous sea, the barque *Viking*, of Sunderland, with a cargo of coal from Cardiff for the Mediterranean, had been unable to round Trevose Head in the severe conditions, and in a desperate attempt to save lives as well as his ship her master headed for the sandy beach of Harlyn, where, despite the heavy surf, he believed there was a better chance of survival than on the rocks. As soon as the barque had been seen in danger, the lifeboat crew hurried to the Cove to put into practice what had been often tried at quarterly exercises. They launched the boat and brought her back to Padstow while ten horses had been obtained and used to bring the carriage from its house in the town to the outer slip. The boat was hauled onto the carriage and the team started along the quay, taking the hill at a gallop, and when the speed slowed many willing helpers pushed and pulled. Once out of Padstow, the pace quickened again and boat and carriage were soon at Harlyn Bay, where the barque was now ashore but some distance off. Three men had tried to swim ashore in desperation, and had been saved by brave spectators dashing into the surf.

The water was shallow, and the gale right on shore, bringing in very heavy breakers, so launching required considerable efforts, but the boat was got afloat. She was filled by the first breaker, and as the crew strained at the oars against the sea and the gale their progress was so slow that many thought they would be beaten back. But they slowly crept forward and reached the wreck, which was lying bows-on offering almost no shelter. So the lifeboat had to be kept under the bowsprit by means of a single line and constant use of the oars, while seas repeatedly swept the length of the barque and into the lifeboat. The mate first came down the line with a bundle in his coat, which proved to be the master's baby. The baby was taken by the bowman and handed back into the boat, but the mate missed his hold and was swept away to drown. At that moment the rope parted and a succession of seas forced the lifeboat back to the shore. The baby was landed at this opportunity and again the crew battled back to the wreck to take off the master, his wife and boy, and three others. The cook refused the lifeboat, but lashed himself to a ladder and jumped overboard. He was washed ashore and had to be revived using artificial respiration. For their oustanding efforts during this service, Silver medals were awarded to Coxswain William Corkhill and Second Coxswain S. Bates.

In 1874 the lifeboat undertook four launches in less than a month. The first was on 20 November, when the lifeboat went out to help the schooner *Topaz*, of Glasgow, in a violent gale. The schooner managed to come in safely on her own, with the lifeboat standing by. Nine days later the lifeboat was launched to the Waterford schooner *Huldah* which, bound from Southampton for Cardiff, lost her sails in a strong north-westerly gale, so made for Padstow. As she entered harbour she was reached the edge of the Doom Bar before her anchors held. The ebb tide kept her broadside to the gale and very heavy seas were breaking over her when the lifeboat took off her crew of five. Soon afterwards she dragged across the sand and was smashed to pieces on the rocks at Trebetherick.

On the afternoon of 9 December 1874 the British and Irish Steam Packet Company's steamer *Countess of Dublin* fell in with a dismasted brig about fifty

The Padstow lifeboat crew pictured at Hawker's Cove in 1899. (By courtesy of Padstow RNLI)

miles south-west of the Smalls. She was seen to be abandoned, but still apparently sound, so McCarthy, the mate, and five men boarded her to try and bring her to port. She was the brig *Thomas,* of Whitehaven, built in 1800, laden with sulphur ore, and the steamer towed her to port after a hawser had been secured. In the stormy weather the warp parted, and after two others parted in quick succession Countess was forced to stand by in an increasing gale hoping to recover her men. No opportunity presented itself during the rest of that night to recover the men, and throughout the next day the steamer tried to keep the worst of the seas from *Thomas*, which was helplessly wallowing in the troughs. As darkness fell, with squalls of rain, they suddenly lost the brig and despite searching could not find her again, concluding that she had foundered.

Although the brig had not sunk, those on board had lost sight of the steamer's lights and McCarthy realised that their safety now depended on their own resourcefulness. He set as many rags of sail as he could improvise, and thus gained some steerage, setting course for Padstow harbour. Having drifted towards the Cornish coast for a day and a night, they were not surprised when, only an hour later, they saw the light of Trevose. Although they now knew their position, they realised they were heading for a lee shore in a vessel over which they had limited control. But McCarthy's seamanship was excellent and he managed to keep away from the coast, getting a little shelter between Gulland and Newland Islands, and there, at 5am on 12 December, they dropped anchor. Their lights were seen by the Coast Guard and at dawn the lifeboat crew was summoned.

The lifeboat was launched immediately, manned by Coxswain William Corkhill, second Coxswain Samuel Bate, Richard Fradd, James Brabyn, John Randall, William Hellyar, Thomas Ivey, William Brown, William Webb, John Truscott, William Cowl, William Henry Brabyn, James Harris, and Commander Aitchison, Inspecting Officer of the Coast Guard. They pulled out of the harbour against the northerly gale, through heavy seas, and reached the brig to find her pulling at her anchor cables. The six men were taken off one by one, after which the lifeboat pulled away with the drogue streamed aft, and she sped back to the harbour. The day after the rescue, *Thomas* was seen still at anchor, so, with the weather improving, the local paddle tug *Amazon* towed the lifeboat out again. A hawser was passed across to the derelict vessel, a couple of lifeboat men boarded her and made the rope fast, and she was towed into harbour.

The following year *Albert Edward* undertook a couple of services, the first on 26 September 1875, when she rescued the crew of eight of the brigantine *Immacolata*, of Naples, which was caught outside Padstow Bar in heavy breaking seas in a south-westerly gale, and before midnight *Immacolata* had become a total wreck. On 6 November *Albert Edward* went to the French brig *Marie Josephine*, of Cherbourg, bound from Swansea to Caen, which had stranded on the Doom bar. The lifeboat saved four men who had been left on board by the rest of the crew in a north-westerly gale. At the end of 1876, the Silver Second-Service clasp was awarded to Coxswain William Corkhill on his retirement from the crew and in acknowledgement of 'his long and valuable services to the lifeboat'.

On 20 February 1877 *Albert Edward* was involved in helping three different

vessels, with the first seen at about 8am. She was the schooner *Jeune Prosper*, bound from Swansea to Bordeaux, running before a strong north-westerly gale for Padstow Harbour. The lifeboat was quickly launched, but before she had reached the casualty, the schooner struck on the Doom Bar, and then, falling off into deep water, capsized, leaving the crew in the water. Two were drowned but two were picked up by a pilot vessel, and one was saved by the lifeboat. Just as the lifeboat returned to her station another vessel, the French lugger *St Clement*, from Cardiff, bound to Nantes, was seen running for the harbour, and this time the lifeboat was able to pilot her past the dangers of the Bar and to a safe anchorage. During this service the coxswain saw the schooner *Plymouth* part her anchors in the gale, so the lifeboat immediately went to help and succeeded in rescuing four persons from this wreck, which stranded and sank.

There were three more services in the last quarter of 1881, the first on 14 October when the lifeboat put off in a strong north-westerly gale and very heavy seas to rescue, with great difficulty, the crew of four from the schooner *Favorite*, of Quimper, which had lost her sails and had stranded on the Doom bar. The weather afterwards moderated, and on the next tide the vessel beat over the sand. Five days later, at about 11am, a ketch, *Two Brothers*, of Bridgwater, from Newport to Boscastle, was seen in difficulty during a strong south-easterly gale trying to make the harbour. She had lost her sails and let go her anchors about a mile below Stepper Point, in a dangerous position. At about 7pm the lifeboat was launched, and after an hour and a half pull, succeeded in reaching her, and brought her crew of three men ashore. The final service of the year saw *Albert Edward* standing by the barque *Milka*, of Fiume.

In 1882 a number of changes were made at the station. The lifeboat slipway was repaired at a cost of £15 and soon afterwards the RNLI offered the crew a new lifeboat. As they strongly attached to *Albert Edward* at first they refused, but in August the committee and crew agreed to accept the offer. On the personnel side, the RNLI voted the Thanks Inscribed on Vellum to the Rev R. Tyacke on

Arab lifeboat of 1883 during a practice launch in Harlyn Bay, using the carriage kept in the carriage house. (By courtesy of Padstow RNLI)

2 February 1882 after he resigned as Honorary Secretary having been in the post for twenty-seven years, becoming Secretary when the RNLI took over the station. In 1883 the Silver medal was awarded to William Webb on his retirement as coxswain 'in recognition of his gallant services during the past thirteen years'.

What proved to be the last service of *Albert Edward* was undertaken on 1 February 1883 when she launched at 9.30pm to the schooner *Mary Josephine*, of Padstow, bound from Padstow to Hayle with slate, and brought her crew of three men ashore. The schooner was in a dangerous position, about half a mile from Stepper Point, and had been caught out in bad weather, but fortunately her anchors held. *Albert Edward* was replaced in August 1883 by the new lifeboat and, somewhat unusually, was later sold to Mr Preston, the donor of the new boat, for £10. During almost twenty years on station, she distinguished herself in saving more than 106 lives and launching thirty-three times on service.

The first Arab lifeboat (1883-1900)

Lifeboat design had advanced since the 1860s, and so the new ten-oared 34ft self-righter built for the station was of an improved design compared to *Albert Edward*. The new boat was funded by Mr R.A.B. Preston, a barrister, whose own yacht, *Arab*, had been wrecked in the English Channel. Bound from Boulogne for Dover on 24 October 1882, the vessel was caught in a south-westerly gale on the southern part of the Goodwins and became a total wreck from which the owner and eight friends were saved by the Ramsgate lifeboat, which had been towed to the scene by the tug *Aid*. Mr Preston offered £1,000 to provide a new lifeboat station in gratitude for being saved, and his money provided not only the new lifeboat at Padstow but also the new carriage house.

The carriage house, an unusual and unique development, was built in Trethillick Lane, about half a mile from the town. Because they were light enough to be carriage launched, and because sailing against the wind in a vessel

Arab completed her harbour trials in London and was exhibited in Hyde Park before being shipped to Falmouth. She is pictured on her launching carriage at St Columb Major on 15 August 1883 on the final leg of her journey from Truro to Padstow. (By courtesy of Padstow RNLI)

relying solely on manpower was slow and exhausting work, pulling and sailing self-righting lifeboats would sometimes be taken further afield to be launched from a location that would enable the casualty to be reached more easily, such as Harlyn Bay in the case of Padstow. So the carriage was intended to be used to move the lifeboat from Hawker's Cove, where it was launched over skids, to the best location to assist a casualty. The new building, of a simple design, was constructed by Mr Prideaux Brune's workmen at a cost of £258 14s 10d, while £40 11s was paid to G. Davis for iron work, and it was ready in 1884. The carriage that it housed was used mainly during exercises and was rarely needed for services; the house remains standing, albeit in a somewhat overgrown state.

The new lifeboat, built by Woolfe at Shadwell, was ready In June 1883, having satisfactorily completed her harbour trial. She was named after the donor's yacht, and before leaving London for Padstow took part in trials on the Serpentine as part of the International Fisheries Exhibition. She left London on 10 August 1883 for Truro, transported by the Great Western Railway, and from there was taken by

A postcard entitled 'Padstow Lifeboat crossing the Doombar in a gale', showing Arab under oars.

Arab (1883) afloat at Hawker's Cove. (By courtesy of Padstow RNLI)

road on her carriage to Padstow. On her arrival on 15 August, she was drawn on her carriage by 'eight sturdy greys' and was met by 'a vast concourse of people', as a contemporary account reported. During the inauguration ceremony held that day, she was named by Mr Preston's wife and was afterwards launched for a demonstration. The crew were, according to the District Inspector, 'well satisfied with the good qualities of their new boat'.

Within three weeks *Arab* was called out on her first service, launching on 3 September 1883 to the schooner *Maria*, of Granville, which was bound for that port from Swansea, with a cargo of coal, and had stranded on the Doom Bar in a strong westerly wind and high seas. The tide was ebbing and, although seas broke completely over his craft, her master, a man named Roullet, refused all offers of help, thinking he would be safe until the next tide refloated his vessel. However, when the tide rose in the afternoon the situation became increasingly dangerous, with three of his crew managing to get ashore in their boat. This was seen by the lookout and at 2pm *Arab* was launched to take off the master and one remaining hand. Some gigs took hawsers from the Stepper Point capstans to the schooner, but before they could provide any assistance the casualty heeled over and sank, later becoming a total wreck.

On 10 October 1884 the schooner *Eliza*, of Penzance, homeward bound from Porthcawl, sprung a leak after being caught in a strong north-westerly gale and had to make for Padstow. She was not fully under control as she entered the harbour, and was soon swept on to the edge of the Doom Bar, where she lay with the seas breaking over her. Within forty minutes the lifeboat was manned, launched, got to the sands, took off the five crew, and landed them at the Cove.

The next service, which came two years later, was another involving a vessel on the Doom Bar, but on this occasion the whole crew was not saved. In the late evening of 17 October 1886 the Norwegian barque *Alliance*, with a cargo of timber from Halifax, Nova Scotia, for Glasgow, was seen labouring off Gulland in a strong north-westerly gale with breaking seas, flying a signal of distress. A messenger from Trevose was sent on horseback to Hawker's Cove to warn the Coxswain, and while the lifeboat was being prepared the messenger went to Padstow to get the crew. The barque meanwhile, buffeted by the gale, was making for the harbour, but after being caught in a squall which took away some of her sails, she was driven on to the Doom Bar. With heavy seas sweeping her decks, she heeled over and almost immediately her main and mizen masts fell, taking with them four of the crew, who were drowned. When the lifeboat *Elizabeth Moore Garden*, which had served at Bude and was at Padstow on temporary duty, arrived, the opportunity was taken to get under the casualty's lee so that the remaining seven men could be dragged aboard. The lifeboat was then pulled to the comparatively sheltered water under Stepper Point and soon afterwards reached the safety of Hawker's Cove.

Arab returned to station after various alterations had been made in 1889 and on 14 January 1890 she assisted to save the ketch *Charles Francis*, of Plymouth. Later in the year, on 7 November 1890 she went to another Norwegian timber ship, which was carrying Baltic deals destined for Bridgwater, the brigantine *Helios*, of Tonsberg, which was seen up-Channel, unable to prevent herself drifting to leeward in a north-westerly gale. Rather than get caught on the shelterless coast to the north, she altered course and made for Padstow. The lifeboat was launched as soon as this change of course was noticed by those on shore, and she might have reached the casualty before disaster struck, but she

Arab (1883) afloat at Hawker's Cove, with a full crew on board, returning from exercise. (By courtesy of Padstow RNLI)

The 34ft self-righter Arab, on station 1883 to 1900, launching from the boathouse at Hawker's Cove. The first RNLI lifeboat (1856-64) and the earlier Harbour Association lifeboat were kept in the lower part of the house on the left.

shortened sail as she rounded Stepper Point, lost way and, her anchors not being ready, was driven onto the Doom Bar. The lifeboat, having been swept by several heavy seas in the course of a hard pull seawards, reached her just after she struck and took off her crew of seven.

Two services were performed in 1894. On 13 January *Arab* rendered assistance to the ketch St *Petroc*, of Padstow, whose master needed the assistance of more men or a tug, but only a small tug was available, and it was unsafe for her to go out in the prevailing seas. Five men volunteered for the service and were taken off by the lifeboat, which remained by the vessel until sail was set and the tug was able to take her in tow. The other service of the year was undertaken on

24 April after the yawl *Oneida*, of Sennen Cove, which had left Padstow in the morning to pick up her nets, got into difficulty in a strong south-westerly gale with a heavy ground sea. The crew, finding they could not return to Padstow, attempted to anchor their boat, but when the anchors did not hold, the men signalled for help. *Arab* launched at 3.15pm and, on reaching the vessel, found that her crew of three thoroughly exhausted so they took the yawl in tow and brought her into harbour just over an hour after launching.

The year 1895 proved to be the busiest for *Arab* during her time at Padstow, with the first service undertaken during the morning of 2 January when she saved four from the barque *Antoinette*. Earlier, ten of the barque's crew had been saved by the Port Isaac lifeboat, which had escorted the casualty up the coast. In the afternoon of the same day five men put off in a gig to try and save the barque itself, but in the heavy ground seas they found themselves in considerable danger. As they could not use their own boat to get back to shore, Arab was launched and brought them to safety, after which *Antoinette* filled with water and became a total wreck. On 14 February *Arab* went to the ketch *Tavy*, of Plymouth, which entered the harbour at 7pm but was unable to take a pilot because of the heavy seas and south-easterly gale. She anchored off Hawker's Cove, but needed help after she began to drag her anchors. Her crew of four were saved by the lifeboat and the ketch became a wreck on the rocks. The next service was undertaken on 29 March when *Arab* stood by the schooner *Lizzie Treriberth*, of Fowey, which had been caught in a strong north-westerly gale and heavy seas. The vessel managed to anchor safely inside the Point after which the lifeboat, towed by a steam tug, returned to Hawker's Cove.

The last services of 1895 were performed on consecutive days and resulted in two fine rescues. At first light on 2 October a vessel was seen with its mast and sails blown away by the strong north-westerly gale. *Arab* launched at 6.35am and found that the ketch *William*, of Ipswich, bound from Swansea for Wells, in

The crew of Arab, pose for the camera. On the extreme left is Coxswain Davd Grubb, wh was later Coxswain of the ill-fated James Stevens No.4. (By courtesy of Padstow RNLI)

The 34ft self-righter Arab being hauled down the slipway at Hawker's Cove ready for launching. She served the station until being wrecked on service on 11 April 1900.

difficulty. She had drifted towards the harbour, anchoring just clear of the Doom Bar, but was disabled and in the difficult conditions salvage was impossible, so the lifeboat landed the four crew. The lifeboat then stood by in case the ketch could be saved, but before noon her anchor chain parted and she was driven over the sands on to Trebetherick rocks, where she soon broke up.

The next day, with the gale continuing, a ship's boat was seen approaching the harbour at about noon. The lifeboat launched and went to the boat as it rounded Stepper Point, and the Coxswain was informed that another boat, with sixteen men on board, was still adrift having left the steamer *Sicilia*, of Liverpool, which had been wrecked west of Trevose. Arab immediately headed out to sea, but on rounding Stepper Point, and facing the full force of the gale, the crew found they were unable to make headway, and were eventually driven back by the wind and waves. Coxswain Grubb decided to return for a fresh crew, changing three of the older members who were exhausted. On this attempt, the lifeboat did get out to the open sea and, in spite of the driving spume, saw the boat much closer to the shore than expected, in Hell Bay, and in a very dangerous position. The lifeboat changed course and pulled towards the casualty, helped by the wind, and saw that the survivors were exhausted. They were reached just in time and quickly taken aboard the lifeboat. Now heavily laden, the lifeboat struggled the considerable distance to leeward of the harbour against the weather, but they safely reached the shore.

The Steam Lifeboat

Towards the end of the nineteenth century the RNLI investigated the possibility of operating steam-powered lifeboats. At a number of the major ports on the east coast, notably Ramsgate, Gorleston and Harwich, pulling and sailing lifeboats worked in conjunction with a steam-powered tug, which towed to the scene of a rescue. Many coxswains and crews regarded this as an ideal arrangement, as the close-quarters manoeuvrability of a pulling lifeboat when attending a wreck was better than that of a larger and somewhat cumbersome steam tug, which itself was ideal in getting to a distant casualty.

However, a steam lifeboat, operated by the RNLI and thus ready specifically for life-saving duties, would offer advantages over a lifeboat relying on sails or oars, and over the steam tug and pulling lifeboat combination. By the 1880s steam had been used for many years to power ships of all sizes, but doubts existed about the efficiency of steam-powered craft when used for life-saving, and building a steam powered lifeboat presented lifeboat designers with a difficult set of challenges to those of pulling lifeboat design. However, the advantages it offered convinced the RNLI to go ahead with construction and designs

The RNLI's first steam lifeboat, Duke of Northumberland, was built in 1889 and is pictured on trials in the early 1890s before going on station at Harwich. (By courtesy of the RNLI)

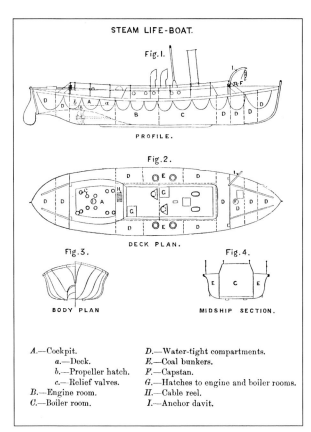

STEAM LIFE-BOAT.

Fig. I.

PROFILE.

Fig. 2.

DECK PLAN.

Fig. 3.

BODY PLAN

Fig. 4.

MIDSHIP SECTION.

A.—Cockpit.
  a.—Deck.
  b.—Propeller hatch.
  c.—Relief valves.
B.—Engine room.
C.—Boiler room.

D.—Water-tight compartments.
E.—Coal bunkers.
F.—Capstan.
G.—Hatches to engine and boiler rooms.
H.—Cable reel.
I.—Anchor davit.

A generic plan of the steam lifeboat which appeared in the RNLI's Annual Reports circa 1900-27. It shows screw propulsion and the mast after the funnel, as on James Stevens No.4.

for a mechanically-drive lifeboat were examined. A design by the London-based boatbuilder Messrs R. and H. Green, of Blackwall, submitted in June 1888, was subsequently deemed most suitable and the company was ordered to build a steam lifeboat to plans provided by the RNLI and based on modified versions of those envisaged by Greens.

The prototype steam lifeboat was completed in 1889 and made her first trial trip on 31 May 1889. Named *Duke of Northumberland*, she was fitted with a Thornycroft engine which, with its 'patent tubulous pattern' boiler, produced 170hp and drove hydraulic pumps, which were in effect water jets. She was 50ft in length, had a moulded breadth of 12ft and an extreme breadth of 14ft 3¾in. On 4 August 1890 she was taken to the Maplin measured mile for speed trials, averaging more than nine knots. With a full bunker of three tons of coal, her radius of action was 254 miles at a speed of eight and a half knots.

Duke of Northumberland was the first of six steam lifeboats built by the RNLI, all of which were over 50ft in length. Although they could cover a much greater area than any pulling or sailing lifeboat, their size restricted the number of places where they could be stationed as they had to be kept moored afloat, and, unlike today, fewer places existed where sheltered moorings could be taken up. In Cornwall, Padstow was deemed the only suitable place from where such

The steam lifeboat James Stevens No.4 was twin funnelled and powered by twin screws. (By courtesy of Padstow RNLI)

A rare photograph of the steam lifeboat James Stevens No.4 getting up steam. (By courtesy of Padstow RNLI)

a vessel could operate and one was sent to the station in 1899 in response to two disasters in March 1897 when the steamer *Siracusa*, of Hamburg, and the Newquay-owned ketch *Engineer* were lost with all hands. In both cases the Newquay pulling lifeboat did all that was possible in terrible weather conditions, but, it was believed by locals, these casualties might have been helped, perhaps even avoided, had a powered lifeboat been available. Both Newquay and Padstow committees applied to have steam lifeboat, but in the former case it would have necessitated expensive harbour works to provide the necessary shelter, so, at a Committee Meeting on 8 April 1897, a few weeks after the Padstow committee's letter and recommendations, the RNLI decided to have a steam lifeboat built for the station as soon as possible.

The steam lifeboats were still largely experimental at this time, and whereas the first three employed hydraulic jet propulsion, as it was believed this was less

James Stevens No.4 passing Stepper Point on her way to the ketch Peace and Plenty. (By courtesy of Padstow RNLI)

The trawling ketch Peace and Plenty wrecked on the rocks in April 1900. Three of her crew were drowned. (Grahame Farr, by courtesy of RNLI)

vulnerable than a screw, jets were found to have certain drawbacks, mainly a tendency for the outlets to be choked with seaweed. As a result, the new Padstow boat, one of twenty of various types funded from a large legacy left to the RNLI by James Stevens of Birmingham, was screw-propelled and named *James Stevens No.4*. Measuring 56ft 6in in length, 14ft 8in in beam and of thirty-one tons displacement, she was only the second lifeboat to be built that was driven by a single propeller, with her sistership, *James Stevens No.3*, being the first. She was fitted with compound engines and a patent water-tube boiler which gave her a speed of 9.3 knots. She arrived at Padstow in February 1899, and David Grubb, who had commanded *Arab* since 1892, was appointed her Coxswain. Her crew was eleven in total, of whom the two engineers and two firemen were permanent employees sent to the station with the boat.

Within a few weeks of her arrival, *James Stevens No.4* was called into action, launching on the afternoon of 7 April in a strong north-westerly gale with heavy seas and rain squalls to a vessel in distress off Tintagel, an area that would hitherto have been covered by the Port Isaac pulling lifeboat. This was a good opportunity to test the efficiency of the new arrangements and, once the call had been received, the steam lifeboat soon left her moorings and headed north. During the passage, she mounted the waves easily, but on a few occasions was buried by them. One of the waves carried away a light board and some deck fittings, but the boat's general manoeuvrability and power were more than satisfactory. The lifeboat soon arrived on scene, but after an extensive search could find no vessel needing help and so returned to station. However, as the boat entered the Camel estuary she found the brig *Emilie*, of Redon, being towed by a steam tug, neither of which could make headway, so the lifeboat took a rope and together the two steam boats towed the brig to an anchorage at Hawker's Cove.

On the same afternoon the pulling lifeboat *Arab* was called out to the ketch *Fairwater*, of Jersey, coal laden from Cardiff, which was running for the harbour flying a signal of distress. On reaching the mouth, the ketch was caught in the eddy winds and currents and drifted unmanageably to the breakers at the back of the Doom Bar. *Arab* was launched at 4pm and was rowed to the casualty, taking off the crew of four. The ketch later drifted into Hell Bay and became a total wreck, while *Arab* was back on station just eighty minutes after launching.

Sadly, *James Stevens No.4* only served at Padstow for just over a year, completing two services in that time, before she was tragically wrecked in April 1900. The disaster that befell her was one of the worst in the RNLI's history, for not only did the steam lifeboat capsize, but the station's pulling lifeboat, the 34ft self-righter *Arab*, was also wrecked going to the same vessel, the ketch *Peace and Plenty*, of Lowestoft. The ketch, after spending the day of 11 April fishing, anchored at the harbour mouth but by nightfall began to drag her anchors in the strong westerly gale with very heavy breaking seas, and pilots put off to bring the smack in. Before they reached her, however, the cable parted, and the vessel began to drift across the harbour into a dangerous bay. The Trebetherick Life Brigade fired a rocket line to the casualty and managed to drag ashore five of the crew, Harry Catchpole, Branan, Kerrill, Fiske and a boy. Another jumped overboard and made it to the shore safely, but three others, James Jarvis, Henry Hammett and Charles Chapman were drowned. Meanwhile, the maroons were fired to summon the lifeboats, and both the steam and pulling boats put out.

The steam lifeboat James Stevens No.4, barely recognisable, after being thrown into a small cave at the foot of Greenaway Rocks with the loss of eight of her crew in the disaster of April 1899. (By courtesy of RNLI)

The wreck of Arab near the harbour entrance, April 1900. (By courtesy of Padstow RNLI)

Arab launched to assist the ketch, manned by Coxswain Samuel Brown, Second Coxswain William Jermyn, Bowman William baker, and crew members Harold Brown, Richard Bate, Thomas Bray, Joseph Dally, Nathaniel England, George Gill, Samuel Henwood, Arthur Magor, James McOwen and John Pope. She was taken round the edge of the expanse of churning foam that was the Doom Bar, getting over towards the other side of the estuary by taking the narrow channel known as Britannia Way, because of her shallow draught. As she made her way to the casualty in the terrible weather, the ketch was being driven by the gale and the huge seas further over the Doom Bar towards the rocks in Hell Bay and in the darkness and blinding spray the lifeboat crew could see nothing of the ketch. They searched backwards and forwards, but found that in the gale force winds and surf they could make no headway back towards Stepper Point, and forced to stand by for over an hour in the heavy seas waiting for a suitable opportunity to get either closer to the casualty or back ashore and to safety.

Survivors of the James Stevens No.4 disaster: Ernest Tippet, Thomas Grant and Orson French. (By courtesy of the RNLI)

However, as the lifeboat was continuing to search for the casualty, a particularly heavy sea struck the boat, unseated the crew and broke or carried away nine of the ten oars. The boat was completely filled with water, and as this drained away the crew managed to regain the boat, albeit with great difficulty and only by grasping the life-lines, and the anchor was immediately thrown overboard in the hope that it would hold the boat. A distress flare was burnt to tell the steam lifeboat that *Arab* was disabled, and was now in grave danger. As a return to Padstow was impossible, it

was decided to run her ashore at the north-eastern part of the harbour into a small creek in the rocks where it might be possible to beach her. So, using the spare oars, the crew let the anchor drag slowly, and waiting for the lulls between waves, dropped gradually shorewards. They beached the boat and managed to scramble to the safety of the sand dunes, fortunately without any loss of life.

James Stevens No.4 put out through the mouth of the harbour making for deeper water, as her draught was too great for a direct crossing of the sands in the estuary. However, before managing to turn towards the casualty, she was caught by a huge sea, which lifted her stern completely out of the water, and was

Memorials in
Padstow cemetery
to David Grubb
(left) and Joseph
T. Stephens (right),
who lost their lives
in the 1900 disaster
aged twenty-two
and thirty-six
respectively.
(Nicholas Leach)

spun broadside to the waves, being turned over. The seven crewmen that were in the cockpit were thrown clear, but the four men tending the boilers in the engine room were trapped. Three of the men washed off the boat were swept ashore and revived, but tragically the other four did not survive. The lifeboat was thrown into a small cave in the rocks at Hell Bay and was a complete wreck resembling, one onlooker commented the following day, 'nothing so much as a battered tin can'. Those trapped in the engine room were Chief Engineer John Martin, Second Engineer James Old and the two firemen, Joseph Stephens and Sydney East. The other crew who lost their lives were Coxswain David Grubb and crew members Edward Kane, John Bate and James Grubb.

When news of the disaster spread to the county and then nationwide, sincere sympathy was expressed for the relatives of the deceased, and a relief fund was opened for the dependents of the eight men, who left behind four widows and fourteen young children. The RNLI, who reported the event with the 'profoundest sorrow', approved a £1,000 contribution to the fund at a Committee Meeting on 10 May 1900 and also made extra payments to each of the crew of *Arab*, as well as the deck hands, or their representatives, on the steam lifeboat. Pecuniary grants were also made to men who were injured. HM Queen Victoria contributed £25 to the fund and HRH The Prince of Wales £20. The medical expenses of the survivors and of the funerals of the four men whose bodies had been recovered were defrayed by the RNLI. The Board of Trade enquired into the events and cause of the disaster, but could not attribute any fault to the construction of the lifeboat or mismanagement by the crew. But in the space of one terrible night, the station had lost two lifeboats.

The Unique Steam Tug

When considering replacements for the two lifeboats that had been wrecked, the RNLI took an unusual step, as the Lifeboat journal of May 1901 explained: 'Having regard to the terrible nature of the disaster and the exceptional requirements of the locality, the Committee have decided not to replace the wrecked Steam Life-boat, but to substitute for it a sailing Lifeboat to be towed by a Steam-tug which has been specially designed for the purpose by Mr G.L. Watson, the Consulting Naval Architect of the Institution and which is now being built.' This move resulted in the creation of a unique set-up at Padstow with the operation of the only steam tug the RNLI ever built. Commercially operated steam tugs were used in life-saving at other ports, most notably Ramsgate, but as no such tug was available at Padstow, the RNLI built one to their own specification in what was described as 'an entirely new departure' for the Institution. In September 1899 Mr R.A.B. Preston, donor of the lifeboat *Arab*, had visited the station and, following discussions with local officials and crew, wrote to the Institution suggesting, among other matters, that 'a special tug to tow the other lifeboat would be of more service

The steam tug Helen Peele in Padstow harbour. The impressive 95ft 6in twin-screw vessel was designed by George Lennox Watson and represented a unique departure in lifeboat design. (By courtesy of Padstow RNLI)

198. STEAM LIFEBOAT, "HELEN PEELE," in Padstow Harbour.

The large 42ft self-righting lifeboat Edmund Harvey under construction at Thames Ironworks yard at Blackwall, London, in 1901. She was built for service in conjunction with the steam tug. (By courtesy of RNLI)

than the steam lifeboat'. Whether his opinion held sway when the RNLI Committee considered matters following the disaster is not known, but he also brought attention to the fact that the steam lifeboat was 'hardly strong enough for the station', something that proved to be the case less than two years later.

As well as the steam tug, the RNLI provided a new No.1 lifeboat for operating from the Hawker's Cove boathouse and a large sailing lifeboat for working with the steam tug. The smaller No.1 lifeboat, which measured 36ft by 8ft 3in, rowed ten oars and was fitted with two water-ballast tanks, was named *Arab* like her predecessor having been funded by Mr R.A.B. Preston, of London. She was kept on a carriage, newly-built by the Bristol Wagon Works Company, in the house at Hawker's Cove, from where she was intended to cover the estuary and work more closely to the shore than the larger lifeboat. She was fitted with two drop-keels, masts and sails. Built by H. Roberts at Mevagissey on Cornwall's south coast, *Arab* was towed from there by a steam tug which had been specially engaged for the journey on 29 August 1901, and was taken to the North Quay at Padstow, where she was beached, and placed on her carriage at the top of the quay watched by a large number of spectators and admirers, including the chairman, members of the local lifeboat committee and the Honorary Secretary.

The day after she arrived, *Arab* was formally handed over and named with the donor, R.A.B. Preston present. He gave, according to *The Lifeboat* journal,

'a very feeling and suitable address, in which he expressed every confidence in the new Lifeboat which was built by Cornishmen and manned by them, too, who, he knew, would never flinch in their duty when occasion required. Deep as was his regret at the loss of the old Lifeboat, he had the great satisfaction of knowing she had perished on active service, in the performance of her duty, and during her career had been instrumental in saving no less than seventy-five lives.'

He then formally presented the new lifeboat to his brother, Captain George B. Preston, a Member of the Committee of Management, who was representing the RNLI, who in turn handed her over to the local committee and crew. Mr C.G. Prideaux-Brdne, chairman of the local committee, accepted the gift, and the Rev E.F. Nugent led the dedication. As the lifeboat was launched off her new carriage at the end of the proceedings, Miss Preston, sister of the donor, performed the christening ceremony. The new lifeboat was then rowed and manoeuvred to the lifeboat house at Hawker's Cove.

The steam tug arrived at Padstow a few days later. Specially designed by George Lennox Watson, the Consulting Naval Architect of the Institution, she was classed 100 Al in Lloyd's Yacht Register and measured 95ft 6in by 19ft. She was built of steel, fitted with a Scotch boiler and two sets of direct-acting, inverted compound condensing marine engines, indicating collectively 300hp with natural draught, and 400hp collectively with mild forced draught, and these drove twin screws. During her trials, she developed a speed of over ten knots, which was regarded as 'very satisfactory'. Built by Ramage and Ferguson Ltd, of Leith, she was launched from their yard on 28 June 1901, with trials taking place between 2 and 5 September 1901. These proved to be satisfactory, and showed the new tug with her twin screws to be very manoeuvrable when going both ahead and astern, with speed runs also undertaken on the measured mile.

A few days later the tug left Leith and headed south, calling at Southend-on-Sea to pick up the new large sailing lifeboat which had been built by the Thames Ironworks and Shipbuilding Company, and which was then towed to Padstow by the steam tug. The new tug was named *Helen Peele*, her cost having been defrayed in part from a special bequest by the late C. J. Peele, of Chertsey. The larger boat which *Helen Peele* towed to Padstow, a 42ft twelve-oared boat named *Edmund Harvey* after the donor who provided her permanent endowment with a £3,500 legacy, was designated the No.2 lifeboat and was intended for use mainly in conjunction with *Helen Peele*.

A fine photograph of the impressive steam tug Helen Peele at moorings in the Camel estuary.

The steam tug Helen Peele in the Upper Dry Dock at Appledore undergoing survey. (Grahame Far, by courtesy of the RNLI)

The two new boats arrived at Padstow on 15 September 1901, but had a somewhat ignominious arrival as the tug grounded on the Doom Bar as she entered the harbour, fortunately floating off about three hours later without sustaining any damage. *Edmund Harvey's* stem was damaged in the incident, and there followed an enquiry into the grounding. The RNLI's Chief Inspector oversaw the investigation, which ended with the master of the tug being severely reprimanded for 'careless navigation in entering the port and admonished to be more careful in future'. However, this version of events was disputed by the local committee, who attributed the grounding to a failure of the steering gear, which they believed had not been tested properly. Both the steam tug and the large lifeboat were kept at moorings off Hawker's Cove, although initially the tug had to be secured alongside the quay or anchored in the pool as the moorings in the estuary were not ready.

When she had arrived, *Helen Peele* had to have a number of minor alterations made to her: a second spare propeller was added, so she carried both left and right propellers, while a medicine chest was provided at a cost of £5 5s with the tug's permanent crew attending St John Ambulance classes held at Padstow so they knew how to use its contents. This was one of the earliest examples of the RNLI providing first aid training for its crews. The Institution employed a number of crew on a full-time basis to maintain, operate and man the steam tug, with the permanent crew consisting of master, mate and forecastle cook, and the engine room being staffed by an engineer, an assistant engineer and a fireman. The crew were to have various qualifications and skills, with the master needing a certificate recognised by the Board of trade, experience in the management of a steam tug and be 'thoroughly acquainted with the Cornish coast and Bristol Channel'. The master's pay was to be 2s 5d per week, the mate's 1s 15d and the cook's 28d. In the engine room, the RNLI specified that none of the engineers should be more than thirty-five years of age. In addition to the permanent crew, six volunteer deck hands were taken when the tug went out. Henry Richards, aged thirty-one, had been appointed as the tug's chief engineer on 17 June 1901.

These new lifeboats successfully undertook a considerable amount of life-saving work during the twenty-eight years they were stationed at Padstow. The first service performed by *Edmund Harvey* and *Helen Peele* working together took place on 14 December 1901 and proved to be exceptionally testing, especially for the men being towed. The rescue craft put out at 6.30pm into a strong north-easterly gale, rough seas and squally weather. Even in the harbour there were huge waves and the first tow rope broke, forcing *Edmund Harvey's* crew to anchor their boat in the Pool while the tug reconnected the line. When eventually they got past Stepper the crew of *Edmund Harvey* were already soaked to the skin; having boarded the boat at Padstow, they had been unable to pick up their oilskins which were kept at Hawker's Cove. They continued westwards, drenched in spray, and found the steamship *Augugte Legembre*, of Algiers, which was in ballast on passage from Barrow for Port Talbot, with about thirty persons on board. Her steering gear had broken, and she struck the Hats and Barrels, near the Cardigan Bay lightvessel. When the lifeboat and tug reached her, she was sinking, having drifted uncontrollably towards the Cornish coast.

A commercial tug took the steamer in tow, but the rope parted and fouled her propeller, but reconnecting the tow in the darkness was out of the question and so *Helen Peele* faced the gale through the night steaming ahead just sufficiently to keep her station with *Edmund Harvey* hanging on astern. The tug's crew could at least make themselves a meal and hot drinks, but the position of the fifteen men

This picture gives an idea of the extent of the surf enountered in the estuary during westerly gales. On this occasion, 1 September 1908, the steam tug was towing out the lifeboat Edmund Harvey to escort the ship Talus, of Greenock, to safety around Hartland Point. (By courtesy of the RNLI)

The 42ft self-righter Edmund Harvey at moorings in the Camel estuary. She served the station for twenty-eight years and saved seventy-eight lives during that time, often working in conjunction with the steam tug.

in the lifeboat was dreadful. Their emergency rations consisted of chocolate, biscuits and brandy, while they huddled under the sails seeking shelter from the wind and the spray which flew over the bows. The next morning two more tugs arrived and all four commenced to tow the disabled steamer slowly up-Channel, the lifeboat streaming aft. The conditions had improved, with some sunshine, and the slower pace of the tow stopped the waves coming over the bows so that their clothes began to dry. Later in the day, as they rounded Hartland, the sky became overcast and snow fell, with 'their eyes almost blinded with salt, throats sore and dry, and their hands and feet swollen almost beyond recognition', according to historian Claude Berry's account, and they sang Christmas carols. Eventually they arrived at Cardiff at noon on 16 December, having spent forty-four hours at sea, frozen the whole time, soaked most of the time, but all survived the ordeal. The lifeboat was towed back to Padstow the next day by the steam tug.

On the night of 22 February 1903 the steamship *Martha*, of Copenhagen, was reported to be in distress five miles north of Padstow, and was sighted burning signals for assistance. *Helen Peele*, with *Edmund Harvey* in tow, at once put out, and at 12.30am arrived on scene. The steamer had damaged machinery, and the captain requested that the lifeboat men stand by for the rest of the night. Both the lifeboat and tug remained with the casualty and, after temporary repairs had been effected on board the steamer, finding that only a tug was required to tow the steamer to Swansea, they decided to return home. Padstow was reached at 11.15am the next day, the lifeboat men having been exposed to the south-westerly gale and rough and cold weather for thirteen hours.

The first service performed by the smaller pulling lifeboat *Arab* came on 1 March 1903 when, shortly after noon, it was reported that the steam trawler *Birda*, of Milford, was on the Doom Bar with the sea washing over her. While the crew were being assembled the pilots, who were on the spot, with the assistance of their wives and daughters, launched *Arab* in readiness. In a moderate north-westerly gale with rough seas and squally weather, the lifeboat proceeded

to the steamer and managed to rescue the crew of nine men. Later in the day, after the weather moderated, the captain asked to be put back on board again, together with his crew, so that so that they could try to save the vessel when the tide turned. The lifeboat launched again and took the crew back to their steamer and then took a rope to her from the capstan house, which, together with her engines, eventually enabled the vessel to be got off and taken to safety.

Arab was called out again on 13 February 1904 after the trawler *Annie*, of Brixham, grounded on the Doom Bar while attempting to come into Padstow. She was caught by a heavy ground sea and strong south-westerly gale, and as soon as she struck the sands than the seas made a clean breach over her. Within a few minutes Arab had been launched as the five men on board the trawler were in considerable danger, but fortunately before the lifeboat reached them the vessel floated off. By the time *Arab* came alongside they were in comparative

safety. However, the master asked for help to take the vessel into Padstow, and so three lifeboat men were transferred across and helped the vessel safely into port.

Just over a year after this rescue *Edmund Harvey* herself was almost wrecked and was only saved from serious damage by the soundness of her construction after she broke adrift from her moorings during a north-easterly gale on 20 February 1905 and was stranded on the rocks. Some of the squalls during the day were exceptionally violent and the crew of *Helen Peele*, who were on stand-by duty, closely watched *Edmund Harvey*, which was moored astern. At about 3am they were horrified to see her suddenly break adrift and move rapidly towards the lee shore. They launched their own boat, but could not catch the lifeboat before she had stranded under Tregirls Cliffs.

Fortunately the Coastguard had seen the incident and three men went by land, taking ropes and a heaving cane. Coxswain William Baker launched his boat to try to assist. Meanwhile, one of the Coastguard men, T.L. Jinks, was lowered over the cliffs to the boat as it crashed and rolled on the rocks. Despite his precarious position, he was able to establish a towline to *Arab*, which then towed *Edmund Harvey* off and took her up to Padstow quay. At low tide the damage was found to be extensive, albeit superficial, with her stem, bilge keels, side planking and rubbing strakes in need of repairs. She was hauled out of the water at Mr Cowl's premises and the repairs were made under the supervision of an RNLI assistant surveyor. The mooring had broken because a bridle chain had become disconnected from a link, and so alterations and improvements to the mooring were made immediately.

The steam tug Helen Peele at Cowes. (By courtesy of the RNLI)

During 1908 *Edmund Harvey* and *Helen Peele* had a busy year and worked together on four occasions to effect rescues, saving thirty-six lives in the process.

On 8 January the two boats went to the iron barque *Europa*, of Bilbao, which was dismasted and at anchor about eight miles off Trevose Head in heavy seas and a north-westerly gale. Fourteen of the crew had been rescued by the steamer *Everest*, of Cardiff, while a boy had unfortunately drowned in trying to jump across. Seven men remained on board and with considerable difficulty they were rescued and brought to safety. Once on scene, *Edmund Harvey* slipped her tow rope and was rowed under the lee of the barque. Although she repeatedly hit the ship's iron sides, badly damaging her rubbing strake and rails, she managed to take off the Captain and remaining men. Crossing the harbour entrance on their return proved to be difficult for the lifeboat and tug, as the ebb tide conflicted with the heavy seas whipped up by the gale. They had a difficult time lying off for three hours before conditions eased and they were managed to enter harbour, although as she came in *Helen Peele* shipped a heavy sea and some of her fittings were damaged. According to the *Cornish Echo*: 'The crews reported having had a very trying experience, but the boats behaved splendidly.' The Portuguese Lifeboat Society subsequently made rewards to the crew and a medal for the station was sent to Sussex Langford, the Branch Chairman.

The 42ft self-righter Edmund Harvey was one of the largest lifeboats of that type to be built by the RNLI. She was intended for use primarily under sail. (By courtesy of the RNLI)

On 6 March 1908 *Edmund Harvey* and *Helen Peele* were called out at 8pm after a telephone message stated that signals of distress had been reported north-east from Pentire. The lifeboat and tug proceeded to the scene, battling a strong north-westerly gale and heavy seas, and cruised about all night without being able to find the distressed vessel. They then went to within a short distance of Stepper Point, when the Coastguard signalled the position of the vessel, and at 9.20pm found the steamer *Fjordheim*, of Christiania, bound from Venice for London, with a crew of twenty-two. Her propeller was broken and she signalled that she wanted to be towed into safety. Ropes were got on board from the

tug and, accompanied by the lifeboat, the steamer was taken to Barry, in South
Wales, which was reached at 10.35pm on 7 March. Conditions were very testing
for the crew in the lifeboat, who were exhausted from exposure by the time
the harbour was reached. The next day the weather was very bad so the tug and
lifeboat remained at Barry and on the morning of 9 March started for Padstow,
which was reached about midnight.

The third service of 1908 came on 1 September when a large sailing vessel
was reported a short distance off the land with her sails blown away in a heavy
north-westerly gale and tremendous seas through which the two rescue craft
put off at 11am. They found the steel full-rigged ship *Talus*, of Greenock, rolling
severely, caught in bad weather. The ship was watertight, however, and her master
asked the lifeboats to stand by while he made sail and tried to weather Hartland.
Once this had been done, the lifeboats remained on stand by until 9.40pm, when
the weather was moderating, and returned to station at 6am on 2 September.
The final service of the year was undertaken on 11 December when *Edmund
Harvey* and *Helen Peele* saved seven from the steamship *Martha*, of Horten.

Almost five years passed before *Edmund Harvey* and *Helen Peele* completed
another service, but in the meantime *Arab* was busy and undertook a number
of fine launches. On 20 February 1910 she stood by the trawler *New Boy*, of
Lowestoft, until a tug arrived and towed the trawler, accompanied by the
lifeboat, to the town quay. On 1 August 1910 she launched to the schooner *Belle*

of the Plym, of Plymouth, which had stranded on the Doom Bar, at the entrance of the harbour. When the lifeboat reached the schooner, the tide was flowing, so the Coxswain stood by until 10.15pm, when she was successfully towed clear by the local tug.

On 12 November 1911 *Arab*, under Coxswain William Henry Baker, made one of the outstanding rescues in the history of the station. In the afternoon there was a strong north-westerly gale with heavy seas and poor visibility caused by sea mist, when the Belfast schooner *Island Maid* and the French brigantine *Angele*, attempting to enter the harbour, both struck the Doom Bar and were wrecked. *Angele*, which had been running back up-Channel for shelter, was seen in distress off Mawgan Forth by the coastguard lookout, and as she seemed likely to be making for Padstow the Coxswain was informed. While further news was

Edmund Harvey out of the water, with Captain E. P. Hutchings, who served as Honorary Secretary during the late 1920s. (By courtesy of Padstow RNLI)

Arab being prepared for launching at Hawker's Cove, circa 1909. (By courtesy of Padstow RNLI)

Arab being prepared for launching, with the drogue ready on her stern, circa 1909. (By courtesy of Padstow RNLI)

A painting, entitled 'The Padstow Lifeboat' by William Lionel Wylie RA, said to have been inspired by the rescue of the sole survivor form the brigantine Angèle, of Brest, on 12 November 1911 by Arab.

awaited, two men out for a cliff-top walk spotted through the mist a schooner running for the harbour with some of her sails torn. They hurried to the Cove and the Coxswain fired the rocket to summon the *Arab's* crew. The lifeboat launched at 4.45pm and was approaching the entrance to the harbour when the schooner flew round the point, straight on to the Doom Bar. It was obvious nothing could be done to save the ship and so the lifeboat crew immediately took off Captain J.T. Kinch and the five Arklow men comprising her crew, returning ashore little more than an hour after launching.

While they were returning from this rescue, *Angele*, which had a cargo of coal and bricks from Swansea bound for L'Orient, also came round the point, virtually out of control and almost immediately struck the Bar. The lifeboat, having landed the first crew at Hawker's Cove, immediately headed out again into the gathering darkness. As well as fatigue affecting the crew after an hour at the oars in very heavy weather, the fallen tide made the seas even more confused on the sands and the lifeboat had to make a detour to find a deep enough channel to approach *Angele*. Four of the five on the wreck had been washed overboard and drowned, but the Captain, who had also been in the sea, saved himself by grasping a trailing rope. However, the lifeboatmen made every effort to get close to the wreck, but were too exhausted and so the Coxswain decided to return to the station for a fresh crew. The return downwind was comparatively speedy and back at the Cove volunteers were called for.

Although none were forthcoming initially, when Captain Mitchell and

A good photograph of Arab, the 36ft self-righter which served as the No.1 lifeboat from 1901 to 1931, saving seventy-five lives during that time. (By courtesy of Padstow RNLI)

The steam tug Helen Peele taking local supporters for a trip in the estuary. (By courtesy of Padstow RNLI)

Police Constable Turner arrived they at once stepped forward and were soon joined by enough men to make up another complete crew. Besides Coxswain Baker and Second Coxswain William Jermyn, there were the Captain, mate, and two seamen of *Helen Peele*: A. Mitchell, Joseph Atkinson, John Pope and W. Watson respectively; F. Reynolds, J. Horst and W. Cook, all of the Milford steam trawler *Chanticleer*; Constable Turner; J. Fuller and C. Brinham, fishermen; coastguard T. Coles. These men, despite having had no practice in pulling so large a boat, made a desperate effort and reached the now submerged wreck. The Captain then dived into the sea and swam towards the lifeboat wearing a lifebelt. His action made it unnecessary to go alongside, as he explained in broken English that he was the only survivor. The second rescue took only forty minutes. Following this outstanding rescue, Coxswain Baker was awarded the

(Left) William H. Baker served as Coxswain at Hawker's Cove from 1904 to 1923. (Right) Herbert Brown was Coxswain of Edmund Harvey between 1922 and 1929. (By courtesy of Padstow RNLI)

Silver medal by the RNLI and the Thanks of the Institution inscribed on Vellum went to each member of the crew, with a monetary award.

On 30 May 1913 *Edmund Harvey* performed a service on her own, launching during the afternoon to two fishing boats, *Diadem* and *Dreadnought*, that were unable to enter harbour in very rough seas and a strong southerly gale. *Diadem* sheltered under the land, and was eventually able to get into harbour unaided, but *Dreadnought* was driven several miles to leeward, and the fisherman on board more or less lost control of her. It took the lifeboat more than three hours to reach her, by when she was about eight miles offshore. Although those on board were initially reluctant to accept a tow, a line was rigged and the boat was towed to Padstow but, after waiting for the tide, it was almost midnight when the lifeboat returned to her station. The lifeboat had to beat against the southerly

Presentation of the station's Centenary Vellum and Bronze medal to Coxswain W.J. Baker on board Helen Peele, with (below) Arab (on left) and Edmund Harvey alongside the steam tug in the harbour. (By courtesy of Padstow RNLI)

gale throughout the return passage, with the Coxswain afterwards speaking 'in the highest terms of the manner in which she behaved under canvas'.

During the war of 1914-18, the Padstow lifeboats were very busy, with *Arab* performing eight rescues, and *Helen Peele* a further eight, four of which were in conjunction with *Edmund Harvey*. Although no effective services were completed in 1914, during 1915 the lifeboats performed several, the first in January after a vessel was reported in distress about ten miles off Trevose Head. *Helen Peele* put out on 23 January, but in the darkness failed to find the vessel and returned to station. She went out again the next day after a more precise message had been received and found the oil tank steamer *Weehawken*, of Swansea, disabled. The tug, together with two steam trawlers, towed the casualty to Barry, where they arrived at 4.30pm on 25 January. Men from all the craft spent the night at the pumps, and next morning the tanker was safely docked.

The brigantine Angèle, of Brest, which Arab launched to on 12 November 1911 after the vessel went onto the Doom Bar. (Grahame Farr, by courtesy of RNLI)

The No.2 lifeboat Arab going to the assistance of the schooner G.K.C., of Noirmontieres, on 4 May 1913. The lifeboat assisted to save the vessel and her six crew.

On 17 February 1915 *Arab* went out to the steam drifter *True Friend*, of Lowestoft, which was aground on the Doom Bar in a south-westerly gale and moderate seas. The lifeboat took a hawser from the vessel to the shore, and, using the shore capstan, the vessel was refloated. *Edmund Harvey* and *Helen Peele* worked together on 19 March, facing a moderate north-easterly gale to help the dismasted schooner *Frances*, of Lancaster, bound from Plymouth to Swansea. The tug towed the lifeboat to the casualty, which was reached at about 8.30am, and found to be waterlogged, so the five crew were taken off and brought ashore.

Two services were undertaken towards the end of 1915. In the early hours of 2 October *Edmund Harvey* was towed by *Helen Peele* to the ketch *Trio*, of Guernsey, bound for Port Talbot with a cargo of iron and manned by four crew. The vessel was leaking badly with water over her cabin floor and four lifeboat men were put on board to man the pumps. She was then towed by *Helen Peele* into harbour, where she was beached. On 23 December, during a strong south-westerly breeze and rough sea, the schooner *Margaret Murray*, of Padstow, stranded on a sandbank to the east of the harbour. *Helen Peele* put out to try to save the vessel and after several hours of towing, the vessel was refloated and the tug returned to her moorings. *Helen Peele* also went out on 28 December to assist the St Ives lifeboat save the steamship *Taunton*, of Liverpool.

During 1917 *Helen Peele* was requisitioned by the Admiralty for rescue work and was commissioned as an RN tug at Swansea on 29 August 1917. She proceeded to Portland, calling at Padstow and Penzance, for duty as a harbour tug. After being refitted, she assisted in towing the disabled steamers *Leander* and *Wellington*, and also carried out target towing duties for HMS *Amphitrite*. During November 1917 she assisted in refloating the steamship *Alice Taylor* in Weymouth

The steam tug Helen Peele and 52ft self-righter Edmund Harvey, both of which were built in 1901, at moorings off Hawker's Cove. The two boats worked together to effect many rescues until the late 1920s.

Arab alongside Helen Peele in the harbour for the presentation of the station's centenary vellum. (By courtesy of Padstow RNLI)

Arab and Edmund Harvey alongside Helen Peele in the harbour for the presentation of the Centenary Vellum in May 1928. (By courtesy of Padstow RNLI)

Bay and later towed the steamer *Briez* into Portland after she had been holed in a collision with another steamer. From Portland, *Helen Peele* went to South Shields, arriving on 20 December 1917, and going further north to Lerwick a week later. On 8 January 1918 she assisted in towing the trawler *Neath* castle off the rocks and into Lerwick. In February 1918 she was refitted at Aberdeen, and returned to Lerwick on 16 March, from when she was used to assist small ships in distress. She continued at Lerwick until early 1919, when she was released from service. In February 1919 she was repaired and repainted at the Admiralty's expense at Harris Brothers boatyard in Swansea, where the surveyor found the hull and machinery to be in generally good condition, and by early May 1919 the tug had been handed back to the RNLI following the completion of repairs.

Under the Emergency Rescue Boat scheme of 1918, whereby motor fishing boats were subsidised with a view to being available to rescue the crews of wrecked or torpedoed vessels, the Padstow boat made two landings. The first was on 25 May, when seventeen men of a Norwegian steamer were landed from other vessels which had picked them up; and the second was on 8 June, when they landed thirty-four men from the Admiralty collier *Hunsgrove*.

Most of the *Arab's* services during the war were to casualties on the Doom Bar, with one stranding at Gun Point and two rescues in the open sea. On 26 April 1917 she went to the steamship *Heredia*, of Christiania, which had gone ashore. When the lifeboat reached the casualty, the master asked the lifeboat men to search for one of the vessel's boats with five men in. After pulling for three miles, the lifeboat reached the boat and saved the five men. On 23 August 1917 she went off in a strong south-westerly wind and heavy sea to rendezvous with a steamer carrying twenty-four survivors of the steamer *Veghtstroom*, of Liverpool, which had been torpedoed off Godrevy. On 25 August 1918 she was towed out by a motor boat to the French ketch *Republique et Patrie*, which had been disabled after fouling some wreckage. The lifeboat men stood by while a naval patrol boat took the ketch in tow, but as she was leaking badly the lifeboat took off the four crew just before the vessel sank. On returning to station a report came in of a torpedoed steamer and *Arab* was again towed out by the motor boat. She made a search under sail without success, and it was later ascertained that the crew of the steamer *Carasa*, of Bilbao, had been picked up by the Newquay lifeboat.

After the war, rescue work continued, and on 30 September 1919 *Edmund Harvey* and *Helen Peele* worked together to help to save HM drifter *Crimson Rambler*, which had gone ashore in Harlyn Bay. The steam tug eventually succeeded in towing the vessel off. On 7 December 1919 *Helen Peele* went out

This fine photogrph of the steam tug Helen Peele moored in the harbour gives a good impression of her deck layout. (By courtesy of Padstow RNLI)

One of the best known photos of Edmund Harvey, pictured in the harbour with Helen Peele moored alongside the Quay, during lifeboat day in 1909. (By courtesy of Padstow RNLI)

on her own to help save the schooner *Lord Devon*, of Salcombe, which was in difficulties in very heavy seas and a north-westerly gale. A line was got across to the casualty using a life-saving rocket, and the tug then towed the casualty into deeper water and later to Padstow harbour.

The last service before a gap of seven years, unprecedented in the history of this station, took place on 1 December 1921. In the late evening a phone message was received stating that the local fishing boat *Porpoise* was in distress off Harlyn Bay with a broken down engine. It was low tide and the tug could not have got away, but as no time could be lost *Edmund Harvey* put off under sail and found the boat at about midnight, rolling heavily and drifting in a north-easterly gale with rough seas, with her crew of three in need of assistance. The boat was taken in tow and the two vessels were met at sea by *Helen Peele* which towed them the last few miles into the harbour.

The last service before a gap of seven years, unprecedented in the history of this station, took place on 1 December 1921. In the late evening a phone message was received stating that the local fishing boat *Porpoise* was in distress off Harlyn Bay with her engine broken down. It was low tide and the tug could not get away, so *Edmund Harvey* put off under sail and found the boat with her crew of three at about midnight. She was rolling heavily and drifting in a north-easterly gale with rough seas. The boat was taken in tow and they were met by *Helen Peele* which towed the vessels last few miles into the harbour.

Another outstanding rescue took place on 11 February 1928, to the steamer *Taormina*, of Oslo, bound from Port Talbot for Lisbon with coal, which tried to enter Padstow harbour for shelter at low tide in a north-westerly gale and

Another photo of Edmund Harvey in the harbour for lifeboat day in 1909, with supporters watching the boat at the Quay. (By courtesy of Padstow RNLI)

Edmund Harvey in the harbour for lifeboat day 1909, with Helen Peele moored alongside the Quay. (By courtesy of Padstow RNLI)

Helen Peele in dry dock undergoing maintenance work. (By courtesy of Padstow RNLI)

very heavy seas. *Helen Peele* and *Edmund Harvey* were called out, but there was not enough water in the channel for them to reach the casualty, so *Arab* was launched and was pulled by her crew on oars down the channel. At that state of tide she had to cross the dangerous Ketch Bank of the Doom Bar, where she encountered broken water that put her beam on to breaking seas, but she passed through the area safely and managed to get to windward of the steamer, at which point she anchored and veered down. She lay alongside while the eighteen men jumped across from the steamer. The dangerous return journey was accomplished skilfully by Coxswain W. J. Baker, who 'admirably handled' the lifeboat throughout the difficult operation, and 'the good work of the crew at the oars'. An interesting note in the May 1928 edition of the *Lifeboat* journal, in which an account was published, pointed out that of the thirteen in the crew, seven had not previously been out on service. Coxswain Baker was awarded the Bronze medal for this fine service, and each of the crew the Thanks Inscribed on Vellum. The rescue also showed the importance of having a smaller lifeboat with a shallow draught at the station to perform rescues at certain states of the tide.

The medal and vellums were presented at Padstow on 28 May 1928, at the same time as the station was being presented with its centenary vellum. The presentation took place on the bridge of the tug *Helen Peele*, with *Edmund Harvey* and *Arab* alongside and a big crowd watching from the quay. Since 1856 the Padstow boats had rescued 386 lives, while during the century twenty-three silver medals and one bronze medal had been gained by the station. Before the presentation of the Vellum, Captain Charles J. P. Cave, a member of the Committee of Management, presented the Bronze medal to Coxswain Baker, and the Thanks on Vellum to each crew member of Arab for the rescue of eighteen men from the Norwegian steamer *Taormina*. George F. Shee, Secretary of the Institution, then handed the Centenary Vellum to Colonel C. R. Prideaux-Brune, President of the Branch, and spoke 'of the glorious history of

Helen Peele moored alongside the docks at Bristol during a visit to the city. (By courtesy of Padstow RNLI)

the station', adding 'there were few, if any, lifeboat stations where the conditions were so difficult and the dangers so great, and the record of nearly 400 lives rescued in seventy-eight years was greater even than it seemed'. Colonel Prideaux-Brune then handed the Vellum to Captain E. P. Hutchings, Chairman of the Urban District Council, and also Honorary Secretary, to be kept among the civic records of Padstow.

The other service of 1928, which proved to be the last undertaken by *Helen Peele*, presented the tug with the opportunity to take part in another medal-winning service, enabling her to leave service in something of a blaze of glory. At 4.30am on 27 November, in a north-westerly gale and very heavy seas, the Honorary Secretary made enquiries about the local fishing fleet and was told that one was still at sea, *Our Girlie*, of Port Isaac, with five men on board. The coastguard had no news of her, so the tug went out to search. It was still dark, but fortunately her searchlight picked out the missing boat anchored close to a lee shore at Portquin, in great danger, with only one anchor rope holding

The crew of Arab in the late 1920s are, back row, left to right: George Pinch, Frank Bray, Harry Brenton, Bate, Percy Baker and Bill Kitto; front row, left to right: unknown, Jim Soper, John Baker, George McOwen, Walter Bate and Alf Orchard. (By courtesy of Padstow RNLI)

her back from being wrecked on the rocks. There was no time to call for one of the lifeboats, even though their size would have made them more suitable for the rescue, so Captain J. Atkinson decided to make a hazardous attempt to reach the casualty. He ordered oil to be discharged, thus keeping the sea down considerably, and then went to within 200 yards of the rocks, and anchored. The water was shallow there, but he had the cable run out and risked dropping down to the boat, successfully getting alongside and enabling her crew to climb aboard. Even as the windlass drew in the chain pulling the tug back towards deeper water, the fishing boat's cable parted and she was wrecked on the rocks. For this outstanding service, Captain Atkinson was awarded the Bronze medal, the Thanks on Vellum was accorded to each of the crew, and the Thanks on Vellum as well as an inscribed barometer was presented to Captain E.P. Hutchings, the Honorary Secretary.

The two medal-winning services of 1928 were the last before both the Padstow stations were provided with motor lifeboats, as described in the next chapter. At the end of April 1929, the No.2 station received a powerful new boat, and then, in 1931, the No.1 station was given a new light motor self-righter to carry on its work in the estuary. *Helen Peele* left Padstow for the Clyde on 2 May 1929, having been sold out of service to a Captain John Turner to become a yacht tender; what became of her after this is not known. *Edmund Harvey* was sold for £70 in July 1929 and converted to the twin screw motor yacht *Trevone* for a Bristol owner, but was taken to France in the 1990s. By contrast *Arab*, sold in 1931, was used as a coal barge in the Isles of Scilly for a number of years, before becoming a house boat at Looe in Cornwall.

First Motor Lifeboats

Despite the relative success and efficiency of the steam tug and sailing lifeboat working together out of Padstow, by the 1920s the RNLI were making plans to motorise the entire lifeboat fleet as engine-powered lifeboats represented the future. The motor lifeboat allocated to Padstow was the fourth and final boat of the largest type of lifeboat built by the RNLI hitherto. Introduced in the 1920s and built to the design of James Barnett, the RNLI's Consulting Naval Engineer, the 60ft lifeboat was fitted with twin engines and twin propellers, thus eliminating the need for the auxiliary sails that single-engined motor lifeboats carried. Barnett was at the forefront of lifeboat design in the 1920s, building on the work of his predecessor George Watson, and he designed large twin-engined non-self-righting boats, which became the mainstay of the lifeboat fleet for many decades. However, only four of the large Barnett motor lifeboats were built, the last of which, *Princess Mary*, was stationed at Padstow in May 1929.

Princess Mary was slightly larger than the three earlier boats, 61ft in length, 1ft longer than the other boats due to her bow being raked forward. She was completed in 1929 by S. E. Saunders at Cowes at a cost of £14,602 3s 0d. In all

The 61ft Barnett Princess Mary makes an impressive sight during her trials prior to coming to Padstow. (RNLI)

A fine photograph of the impressive 61ft Barnett Princess Mary in the Camel Estuary. Note that none of those on board are wearing lifejackets. (By courtesy of Padstow RNLI)

An engineer on board Princess Mary during her trials. (RNLI)

other respects she was similar to the second and third boats of the class. She was fitted with twin 80hp Weyburn-White six-cylinder petrol engines, and had a range of 310 miles at her full speed of nine and a half knots. Her hull was divided into fourteen watertight compartments, and fitted with seventy air cases. She could take 130 persons on board in rough weather, had two cabins, a searchlight, line-throwing gun, life-saving net and sprays for pouring oil on the waves.

The new lifeboat was funded by a gift to the RNLI, through the Earl of Inchcape, from the Peninsular and Oriental (P&O) group of shipping companies, and was the first response to the appeal which the Prince of Wales made to shipping companies in 1928 to fund motor lifeboats. She was named on 21 July 1930 by HRH Duke of Gloucester at a ceremony presided over by Colonel C. R. Prideaux-Brune, President of the Branch. On behalf of the P&O group, Viscount Glenapp, the Earl of Inchcape's son, presented the lifeboat to the RNLI and she was received by Sir Godfrey Baring, Chairman of the Committee of Management, who in turn presented her to the station. Colonel Prideaux-Brune accepted the lifeboat, and she was dedicated by the Ven M.B. Williamson, Archdeacon of Bodmin. Following the dedication, the Duke of Gloucester named the lifeboat *Princess Mary*. In doing so he said:

'I am very glad to have this opportunity of associating myself with the great work carried out by the Institution which provides and maintains the whole of the lifeboat Service around our 5,000 miles of coast. . . It has never been more efficiently performed than in these days, when the progress of science, especially in the development of the petrol engine, has given new strength to the permanent source of all effective human effort, which lies, of course, in courage, tenacity and self-sacrifice ; and nowhere do we find these qualities more splendidly shown than among the fishing population on our coasts.

'I cannot imagine the launch of any ship, great or small, which better embodies the noblest aim of man than that of a Lifeboat, to use the strength and skill

The Duke of Gloucester at the inaugural ceremony of Princess Mary, 21 July 1930. (By courtesy of the RNLI)

Princess Mary in the harbour at Padstow, possibly after her naming ceremony on 21 July 1930. (By courtesy of Padstow RNLI)

The Duke of Gloucester on board Princess Mary during her inaugural ceremony, 21 July 1930. (RNLI)

acquired after many years of earnest training, in order to go to the help of fellow-men in peril of the sea, without asking or caring whether they be fellow-countrymen or not; and of the perils on this coast the names of Doom Bar and Hell Bay are eloquent proof.

'When Lord Inchcape gave this Boat he thought that she could not have a better name than that of my sister, Princess Mary. When asked, she readily consented to the Boat being called after her. She asked me the other day, on her behalf, to wish Godspeed to the Boat and her gallant Crew. She feels sure that any calls that may be made upon it will be responded to with that bravery and efficiency which have characterised its predecessors. . . . It is with the greatest pleasure that I name this Boat the Princess Mary.'

The Duke then pulled the cord which broke the bottle of wine over the boat's bow, amidst loud cheers from the crowd of wellwishers. During her twenty-three-year career at Padstow, *Princess Mary* launched sixty-three times on service and is credited with saving forty-eight lives. Her first service took place on 8 September 1930, when the coastguard reported a yacht in difficulties off the Doom Bar. She left her moorings at 6.15pm in a moderate south-westerly gale and rough sea, and towed the yacht *Emanuel*, of Bridgwater, to safety together with her crew of two.

Before *Princess Mary* had performed another service, she was joined at Padstow by another new motor lifeboat, sent to the station in May 1931. According to The *Lifeboat* journal, the new boat's duty 'will be to work the inner waters of the Bristol Channel', providing coverage in more sheltered waters. Named *John and Sarah Eliza Stych*, she was a 35ft 6in motor self-righter powered by a single 35hp Weyburn six-cylinder engine, and replaced the pulling lifeboat *Arab*, which

The 61ft Barentt Princess Mary alongside at Bude Canal during a visit for the local Lifeboat Day. (RNLI)

had been operated from the Hawker's Cove station since 1901. Like the pulling lifeboat, *John and Sarah Eliza Stych* was launched down the slip at Hawker's Cove where, to house the lifeboat, a new boathouse and slipway were constructed.

The inauguration ceremony of the new slipway-launched lifeboat took place on 19 August 1931. Built at a cost of £3,754 9s 5d, she was provided from the combination of two legacies, one received from the late John Stych and the other from his wife, the late Mrs Sarah Eliza Stych, of Acocks Green, Birmingham. Mr Stych left some money to the RNLI in 1907 to build a lifeboat to be named after his wife, with the money to be paid on her death. When Mrs Stych died in 1912, it was found that she too had left some money to build a lifeboat to be named after her husband. As neither sum was sufficient for its purpose, the two legacies were combined and invested enabling one lifeboat to be provided and named after the two donors.

The new lifeboat was formally presented by Mr B. Franklyn Stych, and ten other members of the family were present at the ceremony. Sir George Shee, RNLI Secretary, received the boat and presented her to the Branch. The lifeboat was received by Colonel C.R. Prideaux Brune, President of the Branch, and was dedicated by the Bishop of Truro, the Right Rev W.H. Frere. The Rev Charles Plank, Vicar of Padstow, the Rev A. Knight, of the United Methodist Church, and the Rev S. Brown, of the Wesleyan Church, also took part in the ceremony. B. Franklin Stych then named the lifeboat *John and Sarah Eliza Stych*.

Originally *Princess Mary* was designated as the No.2 lifeboat, and was kept

The 35ft 6in self-righting motor lifeboat John and Sarah Eliza Stych on trials in 1931 shortly after she had been completed by the Cowes yard of Saunders-Roe. She was powered by a single 35hp petrol engine. (By courtesy of the RNLI)

The lifeboat house with roller slipway at Hawker's Cove after it had been decommissioned.

at moorings in the harbour, but in 1938 became the No.1 boat with *John and Sarah Eliza Stych* becoming the No.2 boat. This was seen as a more suitable designation as the larger lifeboat undertook most of the services. With the two new motor lifeboats becoming operational from Padstow in the early 1930s, the neighbouring lifeboat at Port Isaac was withdrawn, with the station closing in 1933. As more motor lifeboats entered service, so the number of lifeboat stations in Cornwall was gradually reduced, with the greater range of the motor lifeboats negating the need for so many stations with pulling lifeboats. Despite the reduction in the number of stations, the actual sea area covered by the new motor lifeboats was greater and the danger spots could be reached more quickly than before.

The Padstow motor lifeboats soon proved their worth, and undertook a number of services during the 1930s. During the evening of 4 January 1933 *John and Sarah Eliza Stych* performed her first effective service when she launched at

9.10pm to search for a small fishing boat which was overdue in a south-westerly gale with heavy seas. The boat was found in Daymer Bay, and its single occupant was taken into the lifeboat and the boat was towed back to harbour. Without the lifeboat's assistance, the boat and man would have been lost.

Princess Mary was also in action towards the end of the month, launching on 30 January 1933 to the steamship *Cambalu*, of Liverpool, which had gone aground between Welcombe and Knapps Head in dense fog while bound from Plymouth to Mumbles with a crew of nine. The coastguard at Hartland Point heard her signals of distress and told the lifeboat authorities. Appledore lifeboat *V. C. S.* was launched at 3.15am and *Princess Mary* at 4.45am to search for the casualty. At about 7.40am *Princess Mary's* crew spotted a red flare, and found that the crew of *Cambalu* had abandoned their ship and taken to a small boat, but had been unable to find shore and were still in danger. They were taken on board the lifeboat and, with the ship's boat in tow, the lifeboat returned to Padstow, arriving back at 11.15am. Meanwhile the Appledore lifeboat had been cruising round, but could find no trace of the vessel, and after an exhaustive and fruitless search returned to her station.

The next service by the Padstow lifeboats came during the summer. *John and Sarah Eliza Stych* was launched at 10.41am on 9 July 1933 after a telephone message had been received from the coastguard saying that a small sailing boat was drifting towards Pentire Head. The lifeboat found the old St Ives fishing boat *May Flower*, anchored about 200 yards off Pentire Head, with one man aboard. The boat had left Padstow, where she had been laid up for about a year, but had got into difficulties in a very dangerous position. The lifeboat towed her clear of the headland and then returned to her station.

On the evening of 29 July 1934 the coastguard reported that a yacht was in distress in Constantine Bay in rough seas, so *Princess Mary* put out at 7.10pm. The

Princess Mary at her moorings off the Hawker's Cove lifeboat house. (Grahame Farr, by courtesy of the RNLI)

motor fishing boat *Only Two*, of Newquay, was found anchored just clear of the
breakers on a lee shore, with a crew of four. Both her engines had broken down,
she was helpless and in considerable danger, so the lifeboat crew passed a line
across, and she and her crew were towed safely back to Padstow. The captain of
Only Two subsequently wrote a letter expressing his appreciation of the lifeboat's
services and the kindness shown to him.

During 1935 *John and Sarah Eliza Stych* performed two services, the first
during the evening of 21 April 1935 after a small yacht, anchored in Polzeath
Bay, was spotted in a dangerous position close to the rocks and in danger of
grounding with the ebbing tide. The lifeboat put out at 10.30pm, and found the
yacht *Martlett* with three men on board. She towed the vessel to Padstow, and
returned to station at 11.30pm. The second service came on 17 September when
she went to the ketch *Marie Celine*, of Drogheda, which was dragging her anchor
and unable to start her engine in moderate gale force winds. *John and Sarah Eliza
Stych* put out at 9.13pm and found the ketch just north of Gun Point. She towed
her into Padstow, and returned to station at 10.30pm.

Within the space of five days in January 1938 the two Padstow lifeboats each
performed a service. Early in the morning of 19 January 1938 a boat was seen
near Stepper Point in a dangerous position, and at 3.27am *John and Sarah Eliza
Stych* put out in a moderate westerly breeze and heavy swell. She found the
French fishing vessel *Rostellecois*, of Camaret, which had been in tow of a Belgian
trawler. She had anchored just clear of the broken water off Stepper Point and
her captain asked to be towed out to sea. As this would have been too dangerous,
in case the tow rope parted leaving *Rostellecois* to drift on to the Doom Bar, the

Princess Mary on
her moorings at
Hawker's Cove with
the wreck of the
Fench schooner
Maria Regina on
the Doom Bar. the
schooner, bound
from Laroche
Bernard for Cardiff
with pit props, ran
aground on 2 March
1938. (By courtesy
of the RNLI)

lifeboat stood by, and after *Rostellecois'* crew had got out a second anchor she rescued them and brought them ashore at 4am. *Princess Mary* was called out five days later, during the afternoon of 24 January 1938, to a lighter which was drifting five to six miles north-west of Trevose Head. She put off at 4.30pm and reached the lighter about an hour later, taking the vessel in tow, but it was not until midnight that she reached the inner harbour at Padstow. The lighter was being towed by a tug from Plymouth to Bristol, but the tow had parted early on the night of 23 January and the tug had gone on to Bristol.

In February 1938 *John and Sarah Eliza Stych* was transferred to St Ives to replace *Caroline Parsons*, another 35ft 6in motor self-righter, which had been wrecked on 31 January while landing the crew of the Panamanian steamer *Alba*. As a temporary measure at Padstow, where a motor lifeboat was already in service, the pulling and sailing lifeboat *Docea Chapman* was sent to Padstow. *Docea Chapman* was a reserve boat, built in 1911, and had served at Withernsea and Easington in Yorkshire, leaving the latter station in June 1933 and being transferred to the RNLI's storeyard in London. She remained in store in London until coming to Padstow in December 1938 and staying for just a couple of months. At the same time as this, the two stations at Padstow were renumbered, with *Princess Mary* becoming the No.1 lifeboat. *Docea Chapman* was never launched on service, and in February 1939 she was taken out of service. A month later she was sold locally for £45 and became the fishing boat *Girl Maureen* owned by Tommy Morrisey.

In place of *Docea Chapman* as a No.2 lifeboat another 35ft 6in motor self-righter, *J.H.W.*, which had been built in 1931 for the Lytham St Annes station, was sent to the station. She arrived at Padstow in January 1939 and stayed for eight years, performing a handful of routine services. She was replaced by another second-hand 35ft 6in motor self-righter, *Stanhope Smart*, also built in 1931 and stationed at Bridlington for sixteen years. *Stanhope Smart* stayed for four

Princess Mary on her moorings at Hawker's Cove.

John and Sarah Eliza Stych inside the lifeboat house at Hawker's Cove, with Coxswain William Baker at her bow. He served in the post from 1924 to 1948. (By courtesy of Padstow RNLI)

John and Sarah Eliza Stych launching from the lifeboat house at Hawker's Cove. (By courtesy of Padstow RNLI)

After serving at Padstow, John and Sarah Eliza Stych was sent to St Ives. But in January 1939 she was wrecked on service with the loss of seven lives. She was found after the incident on the rocks near Godrevy. (By courtesy of the RNLI)

The small pulling lifeboat Docea Chapman on the slipway of the Hawker's Cove boathouse. The lifeboat, a 34ft Rubie self-righter, was built in 1911 and served at Withernsea and Easington before coming to Padstow in February 1938, being stationed at Hawker's Cove for less than a year.

years at Padstow and was not launched on service before being replaced, in July 1951, by a new 35ft 6in Liverpool motor, *Bassett-Green*, described below.

Tragically, within a year of being transferred from Padstow, *John and Sarah Eliza Stych* was herself wrecked at St Ives and seven of her crew of eight were drowned. On the same day, 23 January 1939, in the severest gales experienced for many years, twenty-seven lifeboats were launched around the coasts of the United Kingdom. At Padstow, *Princess Mary* was called out at 2am to go to the aid of a small steamer making distress signals about a mile west of Trevose. This turned out to be the former Royal Navy minelayer *Medea*, which had been in tow of the tug Scotsman on her way to South Wales for breaking up. In a north-westerly gale with exceptionally heavy seas, she had broken adrift and bumped over the Doom Bar, eventually stranding at Trebetherick Rocks.

The lifeboat nearly got alongside before *Medea* reached the Doom Bar, but the casualty was buried by a very heavy sea which washed overboard a ventilator and other gear, and damaged the battery, thus putting the lighting system out of action. *Medea* was drifting fast over the sands so Coxswain Atkinson morsed to the Stepper Point lookout man, asking him to report the situation to the life-saving team on the north side of the estuary, then took the lifeboat out to sea to await the tide. Five hours later, when it was safe to enter the harbour, she was overtaken by three successive heavy seas which washed more equipment overboard, filled the canopy and knocked the Coxswain and Second Coxswain from their feet, but the moorings were reached despite the crew being somewhat battered and disappointed, glad to hear that three of the four men on *Medea* had been saved by the rocket apparatus.

With the outbreak of the Second World War in September 1939, conditions in and around Padstow and the Camel estuary changed considerably. And old quarry at Stepper Point was reopened with daily blasting and lorry traffic taking tons of raw material for the construction of an airfield, while a rifle range was established at St Enadoc golf course and extensive sea defences were built. High speed launches were stationed in the harbour and used for air sea rescue work to effect faster responses to air crew who had landed in the water. Many rescues by the lifeboats were to wartime casualties, with the first coming on 19 October 1939 when *Princess Mary* was launched to search for an RAF aircraft reported down in the sea off Bude. The lifeboat had not gone far, however, before a recall message was received. The same sort of frustrating search, often in extremely bad weather, with coastal lights blacked and in bad weather, was undertaken many times during the war. In fact, of twenty-three launches during between 1940 and 1945, fifteen proved to be fruitless.

At 1.50pm on 16 January a message was received from the Stepper Point coastguard that a large RAF launch, which had arrived under Pentire Head, needed help. *Princess Mary* went out in a fresh north-easterly breeze and rough seas to find the launch, whose master asked to be taken into harbour. He had a very rough passage from Penzance, the launch had been slightly damaged, and one of the crew was suffering from concussion having been hit on the head by a falling hatch cover. The coxswain boarded the launch and berthed her in the cove to wait for high water, at which point the lifeboat escorted her into harbour. Later in the year, on 21 August, *Princess Mary* had a fruitless launch, going out to search for enemy aircraft reported to be down north of Trevose Head, but nothing was found.

Between November 1940 and May 1941 the relief *Queen Victoria* was on temporary duty and performed three services. Built in 1929 for the St Peter Port station in Guernsey, *Queen Victoria* was undergoing a survey at Cowes when war broke out and, with the Channel Islands occupied by the Germans, was unable to return to her station. She was therefore placed in the Reserve Fleet and served at Weymouth, Shoreham Harbour and Padstow before going to Killybegs on the west coast of Ireland, where she spent four years until the end of the war. At Padstow, the only service she performed was in the early hours of 5 May after a convoy was attacked from the air about ten miles off Stepper Point, setting

The 35ft 6in motor self-righting lifeboat J.H.W. served as the No.2 lifeboat from January 1939 to November 1947, having been built in 1931 for the Lytham station. (By courtesy of Padstow RNLI)

Princess Mary had a jumping net so that survivors could get aboard more easily from a casualty ship.

one of the ships on fire. The lifeboat put out and found the motor vessel *Marie Flore*, of Antwerp, ablaze from stem to stern. She went alongside the casualty, but the crew got no response to their shouts and all that was found was a ship's boat, which was taken in tow. The lifeboat crew then offered to help the Dutch motor vessel *Narwal*, which was towing another vessel that had been damaged in the same attack, but her help was not needed and, when the vessel in tow sank, *Narwal* rescued the six survivors. The lifeboat then returned to station, but put out again to assist with the search for survivors. She went back to the burning *Marie Flore*, found that the fire had partly died down, put three men on board her and towed her into harbour.

Another service to a convoy was undertaken by the Padstow lifeboatmen on 10 July 1941. At 2.40am the Stepper Point coastguard reported that an SOS was being flashed six miles north-east of Stepper Point and, as passing convoys were being attacked, *Princess Mary* left at 3.26am to investigate. Her crew a ship three miles north of Stepper just over twenty minutes later, but the vessel did not need assistance. The lifeboat returned to harbour and found another ship, *Norval*, with six survivors from the Norwegian steamer *Svint*, of Oslo, which had been attacked. Other survivors were believed to be in two boats ten miles offshore so the lifeboat put out again, and at 5.40am picked up ten men from the ship's boat. One of them was the captain, who wished to go back to *Svint*, but when the lifeboat reached her at 5.55am, she was sinking. The mate was lying dead on deck, so the lifeboat crew brought it his body to Padstow.

A routine service was completed on 17 February 1944. Shortly before noon, the coastguard at Stepper Point telephoned to report distress signals from

Princess Mary alongside the Quay at Padstow. (Grahame Farr, by courtesy of the RNLI)

Princess Mary, pictured at her moorings, was one of the first lifeboats to have twin engines and shelter for her crew.

At the time of her construction, Princess Mary was the largest lifeboat ever built by the RNLI. This excellent photo of her at moorings in the harbour shows well her fine lines. (By courtesy of the RNLI)

a trawler four miles north-west of Trevose Head so *Princess Mary* put out at 12.30pm, finding the Belgian trawler *Atlantic*, of Ostend, with her engine broken down, laden with fish and with six crew on board. At the request of her master, the lifeboat took her in tow, and at 4.30pm the two boats arrived under Pentire Head to await the tide. Permission was sent by the naval authorities to enter harbour at 10pm, and an hour later Atlantic was brought safely into harbour by the lifeboat.

An outstanding rescue was performed towards the end of 1944. On 23 November, at 2.30am, the naval authorities at Falmouth reported that a ship was ashore at Knap Head, near Welcombe Mouth. In rough seas and very heavy, blinding rain squalls *Princess Mary* launched under the command of the Second Mechanic, William Orchard, as he had greater experience than the coxswain and second-coxswain, both of whom had only recently been appointed. Clovelly lifeboat *City of Nottingham* was also launched, and she reached Welcombe Mouth two hours later to find the Norwegian steamer *Sjofna*, of Oslo, loaded with china clay and bound from Fowey to Larne with a crew of nineteen, inside the breakers under cliffs a mile south of Knap Head. The Clovelly lifeboat could not contact the steamer, so stood by until daylight.

Meanwhile, at 6.25pm *Princess Mary* arrived having covered the twenty-eight miles from her station in just under three hours. She found *Sjofna* broadside on and being pounded by heavy seas. Her crew were sheltering in the bridge and, as it was still dark, the acting coxswain decided to wait. As soon as day came, he anchored and the lifeboat dropped down stern first towards the wreck, being swept throughout by heavy following seas, one of which broke on board her, injuring one of the crew. As each sea broke, the mechanic steamed up to meet it, thus taking the strain off the cable. When the lifeboat got near enough, two lines were fire from her line-throwing gun, and although they reached the steamer the crew were unable to secure them because of the heavy seas. So the acting coxswain anchored in a different position, from which he could get closer to the steamer's bridge.

The lifeboat was now so close inshore that she was bumping heavily on the bottom in the trough of the seas, but the crew managed to use the line-throwing gun to get two lines across and this time the *Sjofna's* crew were able to make them fast. Using these lines, a breeches buoy was rigged between the steamer and the lifeboat and seven men were dragged through the seas to safety. Then the line, which had been chafed, was carried away so, as the lifeboat had no more lines to fire, the acting coxswain went out through the breakers to the Clovelly lifeboat, which was standing by, and borrowed her line-throwing pistol. However, as the coastguard life-saving apparatus company had managed to get a line to the steamer from the top of the cliff, to take off the twelve remaining members of her crew, the extra lines were not needed and the lifeboat could head home. She reached Padstow at 3.45pm having been out for over twelve hours, while the Clovelly boat got back to her station at 4.15pm after over thirteen hours at sea.

Following this outstanding service, Acting Coxswain William Orchard was awarded the Silver medal in recognition of the 'great courage and skill in taking this forty-three-ton lifeboat right into the heavy surf'. He was also awarded the Miss Maud Smith reward for courage in memory of John, Seventh Earl of Hardwicke, given for the bravest act of life-saving of the year by a lifeboatman. Further awards were also made, with the Thanks of the Institution inscribed on Vellum being accorded to John T. Murt, Coxswain, and John H. Rokahr, motor-mechanic; a letter of appreciation was sent to the honorary secretary, R.R. Wilton. The acting-coxswain and each crew member received a special reward of £2 in addition to the usual rewards, and the Clovelly coxswain and

Princess Mary at her regular moorings in the Camel Estuary was a well-photographed boat during the 1930s and 1940s. (By courtesy of Padstow RNLI)

crew a special reward of £1 in addition to the usual rewards. A letter was received from the Norwegian Government expressing its most sincere thanks for the Padstow crew's efforts, and, for their outstanding and arduous services during a period of sixteen hours' continuous duty, the Hartland life-saving apparatus company were presented with the shield given each year by HM Coastguard for the best service of the year by the life-saving apparatus.

Nearly two years after this, *Princess Mary* was involved in another Silver medal service. At 10.40am on 12 August 1946 the St Ives coastguard reported that a tug, with a steamer in tow north of St Ives Head, was making little headway in a fresh westerly gale and very heavy seas. When the tug and steamer were seen to be drifting towards the shore, the St Ives lifeboat *Caroline Oates Aver and William Maine* was launched at 2.40pm and set a course for St Agnes Head. However, the weather worsened and the coxswain was forced to return to station, three hours after launching. So the Padstow lifeboat was asked to launch, and in the face of a north-westerly gale, *Princess Mary* left her moorings at 5pm and headed south on a twenty-mile journey battling enormous seas. She reached St Agnes Head at about 8.30pm and found the steamship *Kedah*, of Singapore, three-quarters of a mile east-north-east of the Head, the line having parted from the tug which was towing her from Barrow to Antwerp. Despite having her anchors down, she was dragging towards the shore and was yawing considerably in very confused seas.

The steamer's rescue nets had been lowered down her port side and the lifeboat attempted to get a line aboard, but as the lifeboat approached, *Kedah* sheered away to starboard. At the same time the lifeboat had to go full steam ahead and turn away to meet a huge sea. She then asked for the nets to be shifted to the starboard side and made an attempt on that side, but, just as she came alongside, the steamer again sheered and the lifeboat was swung round by the seas and struck the steamer, causing damage to her own bows. On the third attempt to get close to the steamer, the casualty sheered away again and again the lifeboat was damaged, but the coxswain kept his engines at full speed and this time brought the lifeboat alongside. The steamer's crew of ten were then able to jump into her and she pulled clear at full speed. Despite being badly damaged, *Princess Mary* was sufficiently seaworthy to reach Padstow, arriving there at

Stanhope Smart served as the No.2 lifeboat from 1947 to 1951. Built in 1931, she was originally stationed at Bridlington.

12.20am the following day having been at sea for over seven hours in what were described as 'almost impossible conditions'.

For this courageous rescue, which involved fine seamanship and great determination on the part of the coxswain, and skilful cooperation by the Second Coxswain and the Mechanic, the RNLI awarded the Silver medal to Coxswain John Murt, and the thanks of the Institution inscribed on vellum was accorded to Second Coxswain William Grant, and Mechanic John H. Rokahr; each member of the crew was given a special reward of £2.

The reserve lifeboat *Elsie* arrived at Padstow in September 1946 for temporary duty while *Princess Mary* went to be repaired following the *Kedah* service. The

Princess Mary taking supporters for a trip in the Camel estuary during lifeboat day. (By courtesy of Padstow RNLI)

reserve boat, a 45ft Watson motor type built in 1919 for the St Mary's station, was launched twice on service and saved five lives during her stint in north Cornwall. Her only life-saving service was undertaken on 12 September 1946, when she launched at 7pm to a boat which needed help a mile off Bude breakwater. On her way to Bude, her crew saw a rocket and then, guided by signals from a morse lamp, found the converted fishing boat *Diana III*, of Appledore, with a man, his wife, and three children on board. She was reefed down and had a sea-anchor out. The lifeboat reached the scene at 11.15pm and went alongside to take off the three children, but the man and woman remained on board, and the lifeboat towed *Diana III* to Padstow, returning to her station at 2.38am after a long rescue. The owner sent gifts to both the RNLI and the lifeboat crew following the service.

Princess Mary returned to station following the completion of repairs, and the last six years of her career at Padstow saw her involved in a few largely routine rescues. On 11 May 1947 she went out to a broken down motor launch, with a crew of two, which was being towed by the fishing boat *Patricia*. The rope had parted once and so the lifeboat took over the tow, after supplying the fishing boat with paraffin to enable her to make for Appledore. More than three years passed before the next service, on 17 June 1950, when the lifeboat went out to a naval Sea Otter seaplane which had made a forced landing in Porthcothan Bay, and was attempting to taxi to Padstow. At 4.15pm *Princess Mary* was launched and escorted the seaplane to moorings in Hawker's Cove. And on 30 July 1951 *Princess Mary* searched, together with two aeroplanes, for a small boat which was reported to be in difficulties. One of the aeroplanes reported a cabin cruiser, with two men on board, flying a white shirt three miles north-west of Lower Sharpnose and dropped a smoke float to mark the position. The lifeboat found the boat was running low on petrol, so towed her to the lifeboat station.

In July 1951 a new No.2 lifeboat *Bassett-Green* was sent to Padstow. She was a light 35ft 6in Liverpool type, built by Groves & Guttridge and powered by two 20hp Ferry Kadency FKR3 diesel engines, which gave her a top speed of 7.51 knots. She was funded from a gift from W.H. Bassett-Green, of Winchcombe, Gloucestershire, who had a life's ambition to present three gifts to Great Britain: one to the air, one to the earth and one to the sea. In 1940 he presented a Spitfire aeroplane to the nation to revenge the air-raids on Coventry; to Coventry he also presented a statue of Lady Godiva; and his gift of the lifeboat completed his ambition, with a gift to the sea. The naming ceremony was held on 17 May 1952 when the new boat was dedicated by the Bishop of Truro, the Right Rev E.R. Morgan, assisted by the vicar of Padstow, and named by HRH The Duchess of Kent, who 'wished her and her crew God-speed in their work of rescue'.

The last service by *Princess Mary* at Padstow came on 3 June 1952 after the steamer *British Supremacy* took the ex-motor fishing vessel *Willroy*, of Fleetwood, in tow. The vessel had a crew of three, and she had broken down. She gave her position as thirty-two miles north-west of Trevose Head, and asked for a lifeboat to take over the tow. At 4.20pm *Princess Mary* left her moorings and reached the steamer at 6.40pm, twenty-two miles north-west of Trevose. The lifeboat then towed *Willroy* to Padstow, arriving there at 10pm.

Six months later *Princess Mary* was replaced by a new 52ft Barnett having saved forty-eight lives in sixty-three service launches at Padstow. She was sold out of service in June 1952 to Captain C. H. Harcourt-Smith, RN, of West London, who renamed her *Aries*, and converted her with the aim of crossing the Atlantic in a small boat for the first time in mind. The work was carried out by Tough Brothers at Teddington Wharf, Reddington, Middlesex, with the cooperation of various local firms who presented items of equipment for the ambitious voyage. She was fitted with two Foden FD6 Marine Oil Engines, developing 105bhp, running at 1,800rpm.

The No.2 lifeboat Bassett-Green alongside at Padstow, showing the engine controls and cockpit layout. (By courtesy of Padstow RNLI)

Princess Mary, having been renamed Aries, undergoing alterations before making her historic double crossing of the Atlantic in 1954, thirty-three days outward, eighteen return.

The transatlantic voyage started in May 1954, when she departed from the training ship *Steadfast*, Kingston-on-Thames, taking the greetings of the Mayor of Kingston, England, to the Mayor of Kingston, USA. Crew member David Foden detailed the journey in his log as follows: on 22 May 1954, she left Kingston-on-Thames and left Dartmouth on 26 May, fully stocked; on 19 June, she arrived in Bermuda; and on 20 June, left Bermuda for the USA; she reached New Jersey, USA, on 23 June. The return journey started on 19 July, when *Aries* left Black Island, USA. She arrived at Dartmouth on 7 August and returned to the Thames on 10 August. The outward journey across the Atlantic took thirty-three days from Kingston-on-Thames to Kingston-on-Hudson, the return journey, over 3,000 miles, took eighteen days. During the eighty days that the voyage lasted, *Aries* covered well over 8,000 miles.

In 1956, following the death of Harcourt-Smith, the boat became the property of his executors. They sold her to a Michael Poberejsky, who had her converted in the late 1950s by the French lifeboat builders, Jouett. The rear cabin was slightly raised, and the hull was painted blue. Although she was converted internally, externally she remained as she was originally except for a few minor details. After being bought by Poberejsky, she was taken to the south of France, and used as a private motor yacht at St Jean, Cap Ferrat.

Joseph Hiram Chadwick

n December 1952 a new lifeboat for the No. 1 station arrived at Padstow. Named *Joseph Hiram Chadwick*, she was a 52ft Barnett motor type built by J.S. White at Cowes and funded from the legacy of the late Miss Elizabeth Ellen Chadwick, of Rochdale. Powered by two 60hp Ferry VE.6 six-cylinder diesel engines running at 1,200rpm, she had a fuel capacity for 116 miles at her top speed of 8.79 knots, or 162 miles at her cruising speed of eight knots. The 52ft Barnett class, of which *Joseph Hiram Chadwick* was the fifth to be built, shared a hull design similar to that of *Princess Mary* but, being slightly smaller, was more practical and able to serve at more stations, including those where slipway launching was employed. However, at Padstow the boat was moored in the harbour close to Hawker's Cove, as her predecessor had been.

The new boat had been on station for more than eighteen months before her naming ceremony was held. This took place at the North Quay on 28 July 1954, when Captain Guy D. Fanshawe, a vice-president of the RNLI and member of the Committee of Management, handed the lifeboat into the care of the Padstow branch, and she was accepted by honorary secretary R.R. Wilton. The Rt Rev

Joseph Hiram Chadwick arriving at Padstow in December 1952, with No.2 lifeboat Bassett-Green also in attendance.

Joseph Hiram Chadwick arriving at Padstow on 1 December 1952. She was funded from the legacy of the late Miss Elizabeth Ellen Chadwick, of Rochdale. (From an old postcard in the author's collection)

J. Wellington, Assistant Bishop of Truro, assisted by the Rev P. H. C. Slocombe, vicar of Padstow, and the Rev W. E. Wall, Minister of the Methodist Church, conducted the service of dedication after which Mrs. J. C. F. Prideaux-Brune, president of the Ladies Lifeboat Guild, named her.

Joseph Hiram Chadwick performed her first service on 6 November 1954 after a boat was reported to be on fire in Watergate Bay. As the lifeboat put out at 7.30am in a calm sea, she learnt that the boat was not in Watergate but in Fistral Bay so she made for there and found the yacht *Dawn Star*, of Cork. The boat was not on fire, but at anchor following an engine breakdown, had broken adrift and had gone ashore. Her crew of four had been rescued by a helicopter. Two lifeboatmen boarded the yacht and the lifeboat towed her to Padstow.

For the first ten years of her career at Padstow, *Joseph Hiram Chadwick* was backed up by the No. 2 lifeboat *Bassett-Green*. However, *Bassett-Green* only performed two effective services during her eleven years at Padstow, saving a total of six lives. The first of these services was on 16 September 1955, when she launched to an RAF airborne lifeboat in difficulties off Bude in a heavy swell, a moderate north-west breeze, and flooding tide. Guided by a helicopter, the lifeboat found the RAF boat, which had got into difficulties in the bad weather, in Widemouth Bay. The lifeboat rescued her crew of five and took the boat in tow. However, the boat broke adrift and was taken in tow by another RAF boat, which followed the lifeboat back to Padstow. The Officer Commanding the RAF station at St Eval and his officers made a donation to the Padstow station following this rescue. The other service took place on 19 October 1956, with *Bassett-Green* launching at 8.55pm to the dinghy *Betty*, of Padstow, with a young man on board, which was drifting out to sea. A lifeboat crewman was put aboard the dinghy, which was half full of water, to help with baling, and the lifeboat

John Tallack Murt (on right) with his brother Horace Murt after he had rescued him, January 1958. (By courtesy of Padstow RNLI)

towed *Betty* to Padstow quay. On 31 March 1962 *Bassett-Green* was withdrawn and the No.2 station was closed as it was realised *Joseph Hiram Chadwick* could adequately cover the area. *Bassett-Green* was reallocated to Poole, where she served until 1969, and was then sold out of service.

The services by *Joseph Hiram Chadwick* during the 1950s were routine in nature, and generally she was called out only once a year. In 1956, on 19 August, she helped the yacht *Isle of Rona*, with a crew of two, which was leaking. The yacht was at first escorted, but as she was not making much headway, a line was passed and she was towed to Padstow. And in 1957 the only service performed was on the evening of the 8 December 1957, when the lifeboat went to the Dutch vessel *Tubo*, which was in difficulties twenty miles west of Lundy with her

Joseph Hiram Chadwick moored off Padstow, July 1955. (Grahame Farr, by courtesy of RNLI)

The 35ft 6in Liverpool motor lifeboat Bassett-Green served as the No.2 lifeboat from 1951 to 1962. These three photos were taken at Bristol on 5 June 1961 when she was being put back in the water for her passage to station after being on display at an agricultural show. After Padstow, she served at Poole for seven years and was sold out of RNLI service in 1969. (Grahame Farr, by courtesy of RNLI)

cargo of grain shifting. *Joseph Hiram Chadwick* put out in a rough sea, a north-westerly gale, and made for the position in heavy rain and hail squalls. She found *Tubo*, and stood by until the shelter of Lundy was reached, at which point *Tubo* was able to continue her passage to Swansea without escort.

In December 1957 the reserve lifeboat *Lloyd's*, which had been built in 1932 for the Barra Island station on Scotland's west coast, was sent to Padstow for temporary duty which lasted six months while the station boat went to Falmouth Boat Company for maintenance. The reserve lifeboat was only called out once during her stay, to help the No.2 lifeboat *Bassett-Green* which had launched at 1.25am on the morning of 10 January 1958 after flashing lights had been seen nineteen miles north-east of Pentire Head. *Bassett-Green* put out in very rough seas accompanied by a fresh westerly gale to check the reports of the flashing lights, and searched a large area but found nothing and was recalled at 6.35am. However, on her return passage she developed engine trouble, when about a mile off Boscastle, so *Lloyd's* launched at 8.45am to her aid. Not only was it a case of the larger lifeboat helping the smaller one, but Coxswain John Murt was helping his younger brother, Coxswain Horace Murt. The smaller boat was in a dangerous situation as she was only being held by her anchors in very strong winds, with high cliffs under her lee, which would have quickly wrecked her should she have gone ashore. Fortunately the intercommunicating radio ensured that no time was lost in searching for her and *Lloyd's* went straight to the spot, some twenty miles distant, and took the smaller lifeboat in tow, arriving back on station at 4.45pm.

Joseph Hiram Chadwick returned to station in May 1958 and was soon in action, being called out on 16 May to the motor vessel *Musketier*, of Groningen, which was in difficulty, five miles north of Trevose Head, after her cargo of coal had shifted giving her a twenty-five degree list. The lifeboat put out in a heavy swell and north-westerly gale, finding *Musketier* with the help of an aircraft thirteen and a half miles north-west of Trevose Head. She stood by for fourteen hours until *Musketier's* master reported that the cargo had been secured, enabling the vessel to proceed to Ilfracombe, and the lifeboat returned to her moorings at 4.50pm. The other service of the year came on 29 August when *Joseph Hiram Chadwick* put out in the evening to tow the motor boat *St Minver*, of Padstow, with eight people on board, back to harbour.

A couple of services were completed in 1959, the first on 17 June to the motor boat *Susan Ann* of Padstow, which had broken down off Trevose Head, and the second on 1 October to the motor launch *Empress of England*. The launch was being towed by the coaster *Eldorita* and *Joseph Hiram Chadwick*

The crew of Bassett-Green at the head of the slipway are, back row, left to right: Jeff Twigg, Harry Wills (Winchman), Sussex Carlye, William John Baker (retired Coxswain); front row, left to right: Kelly Brenton (Second Coxswain), Roy Phillips, Percy Baker (Mechanic), Horace Bernard Murt (Coxswain), Dick Bate, John Clifford Murt, and Jack Brenton (Bowman). (By courtesy of Padstow RNLI)

52ft Barnett Joseph Hiram Chadwick served at Padstow from 1952 to 1967 and was the last lifeboat to be kept at moorings in the river off Hawker's Cove. (Grahame Farr, by courtesy of RNLI)

launched at 9.15am to take over the tow, bringing the vessel into Padstow at 3am on 2 October. The lifeboat performed two services in August 1960, recovering a body floating 300 yards north-east of Trevose lighthouse on 8 August and just over a week later bringing in a capsized dinghy and its single occupant.

At 11.40pm on 12 January 1961 *Joseph Hiram Chadwick* put out to the motor fishing vessel *Moonlit Waters*, which had an injured man on board, and had asked for a doctor to be brought to her off Pentire Head. The lifeboat took the divisional director of the British Red Cross Society, as no doctor was available, and met *Moonlit Waters* as arranged. The injured man was transferred to the lifeboat and landed at Padstow at 12.20am on 13 January. The lifeboat then returned to escort the fishing vessel to Padstow and returned to her station at 2am. The other service of 1961 came on 16 August when *Joseph Hiram Chadwick* brought in the motor dinghy *Good Intent* and its single occupant.

In 1961 the RNLI decided to close the No.2 station, partly because Hawker's Cove had been silting up for some years, which made it impossible to launch several hours on each side of the tide. This meant that the larger No.1 boat had been used for practically all calls, and the No.2 boat had not performed an effective service since October 1956. Accordingly the No.2 station was officially closed on 31 March 1962 and *Bassett-Green* was transferred to Poole in Dorset. The No.1 boat had been moved to a more convenient mooring near the Quay at Padstow early in 1961, together with her large boarding boat *William Myatt*, and the light boarding boat. Most of the crew lived in the town, and now the permanent officers also moved there, so that all were at hand when needed.

In 1962, now the sole Padstow lifeboat, *Joseph Hiram Chadwick* completed three routine services, the first of which took place on 3 May when she saved a small sailing dinghy, which had left Newquay at 8.30pm but gone missing, and landed its two occupants who had got aboard a French fishing boat, which was anchored a quarter of a mile south-east of Newquay Head. On 17 August the lifeboat stood by while the Port Isaac coastguard life-saving company hauled two people up cliffs at Polzeath after they had been cut off by the tide. The longest service of the year was undertaken on 15 December when the lifeboat went to help the motor vessel *Nimrod* of Groningen, which had been anchored off Bude with engine trouble since the previous day, and was waiting for a tug to take her in tow. *Joseph Hiram Chadwick* put out at 11.45am in a west-north-westerly gale and a very rough sea, shipping a considerable amount of water on leaving harbour, which caused a partial failure of the radio-telephone.

She found *Nimrod* had dragged her anchors and had drifted three miles south-west of Higher Sharpnose. Her master, Captain Johan Otten, did not want to abandon ship, saying he was awaiting a tug, but the lifeboat remained on stand-by in case she was needed. The Indian motor vessel *State of Rajasthan* attempted to help, and several attempts were made by *Joseph Hiram Chadwick* to pass a line between the vessels, but it proved impossible in the darkness. They lay off, slowly going ahead into the seas, through the rest of the night and until 10am the following day. The Appledore lifeboat arrived to relieve *Joseph Hiram Chadwick*, remaining until next day when the motor vessel *Milo*, of Bristol, succeeded in getting a line to *Nimrod*, and then towing her to Swansea. A letter of appreciation was received by the RNLI from the owners of *Nimrod*.

A series of routine services were carried out in 1964 and 1965. The lifeboat brought in the yacht *Daphne Loo* and her crew of three on 18 July 1964 after the vessel's engine had broken down and she had also sprung a leak, and on

Joseph Hiram Chadwick at Padstow in May 1964 after she had been fitted with an enclosed wheelhouse. (Grahame Farr, by courtesy of RNLI)

9 September 1964 towed a small motor boat, found to be in difficulties off Trebetherick Point, to harbour. On 3 March 1965 she took a doctor out to the Belgian trawler *Sanantonias* to attend to two injured men. The doctor went aboard the trawler and, after examining the men, found that there was no need for them to be brought ashore. And on 15 June 1965 *Joseph Hiram Chadwick* went to the yacht *Sea Ranger*, of New Quay, which needed help off Pentire Point, escorting the yacht to Padstow

On 23 November 1965 *Joseph Hiram Chadwick* undertook the most outstanding service of her time at Padstow when she rescued the crew of two from the fishing vessel *Deo Gratias*. The service began when she was called out just after 4pm following reports that *Deo Gratias* was firing red flares a mile north-west of Kellan Head. There was a westerly gale, gusting at times to violent storm, the sea was very rough and visibility was poor. Conditions on the bar were bad and Coxswain Elliott made for Newland Island before altering course to try to reach the fishing vessel. The Southern Rescue Co-ordination Centre at Mountbatten had diverted a Shackleton aircraft, which had been on a routine training flight, to the area. The aircraft arrived off Kellan Head at 4.40pm and dropped flares which enabled Coxswain Gordon Elliott and his crew to find *Deo Gralias* well to seaward of the position which had been reported, and the lifeboat altered course accordingly.

The lifeboat arrived on scene at 5.10pm to find the fishing vessel riding head to wind with her mizzen set, but this carried away during a heavy squall and the fishing vessel broached, sheering about violently and drifting rapidly downwind. The two men aboard the fishing vessel said they had lost their rudder, were making water and wanted to abandon ship. A line was fired from the lifeboat in an attempt to pass the tow-line, but this failed, as did a second attempt, by when the fishing vessel was settling rapidly by the stern.

View of the Hawker's Cove lifeboat station from Tregirls, with the No.1 lifeboat Joseph Hiram Chadwick at her moorings off the No.2 boathouse. The old Coastguard houses can be seen in the background. (Grahame Farr, by courtesy of RNLI)

The lifeboat house and roller slipway, built at Hawker's Cove in 1931, housed the No.2 motor lifeboat Bassett-Green until 1962. (RNLI)

Coxswain Elliott realised that there was no time to make a further attempt to get a line aboard, so prepared to go alongside, telling the two mechanics that they must respond to his orders promptly, and stationing the rest of his crew forward. He then waited for a lull and put the bow of the lifeboat against the fishing vessel's starboard quarter, which gave sufficient time for the two men to be hauled aboard. The Coxswain then went astern as a heavy sea rolled the fishing vessel under the bow of the lifeboat, which crashed through her bulwark on to the deck. But the lifeboat was able to pull clear and by 6.05pm the lifeboat crew had sent a radio message that they had taken the two men off the fishing vessel and were making for Padstow. The fishing vessel was reported to be adrift and a danger to navigation. Conditions continued to worsen and the coxswain decided to go outside Newland Island and close the Gulland Rocks before turning into Stepper Point. The lifeboat crossed the bar at 7.10pm and

The lifeboat house and slipway built at Hawker's Cove for the small No.2 motor lifeboat. It was operational until 1962 by when siltation made the slipway unusable, as this photograph, taken after the station had close, shows. (By courtesy of Padstow RNLI)

was secured at Padstow quay ten minutes later. The two rescued men, who were suffering from shock, were met by relations and driven to home.

Following this outstanding service, Coxswain Elliott was awarded the Silver medal for gallantry. The crew members were accorded the Institution's Thanks on Vellum; they were Acting Second Coxswain Ernest Murt, Bowman Arthur Permewan, Mechanic William George Pinch, Assistant Mechanic Horace Edward Murt, Emergency Mechanic Philip May, and lifeboatman Arthur May.

In 1966 the continuing siltification of the estuary was proving difficult for the operation of *Joseph Hiram Chadwick*, the problem having already resulted in the withdrawal of the slipway-launched boat, and by the time of the medal-winning service to *Deo Gralias*, the RNLI had decided to build a new station at Trevose Head with slipway launching. During her last two years as Padstow lifeboat, *Joseph Hiram Chadwick* undertook just four more services, all routine in nature. On 26 February 1966 she escorted the Belgian trawler *Combesco* to a safe anchorage, as the trawler was in a dangerous position under Stepper Point in south-westerly gale forces wind and very rough seas.

The boarding boat William Myatt (BB.26) served at Padstow from 1955 to 1965. Measuring 25ft by 8ft, she was larger than standard wooden boarding boats built by the RNLI. She was built in 1931 for the Dover station with a vew to inshore rescue duties as well as boarding the crew on the specially-built fast 64ft lifeboat built for Dover in 1930. (Grahame Farr, by courtesy of the RNLI)

Joseph Hiram Chadwick in the harbour on 29 May1964 during the visit to Padstow by 44-001, the prototype 44ft Waveney steel-hulled lifeboat, pictured overleaf. (Grahame Farr, by courtesy of RNLI)

Joseph Hiram Chadwick performed three services during 1967, her last year on station, the first during the evening of 1 April 1967 when she went to the motor vessel *Vigilante*, which had engine trouble with a sick woman on board and was being towed by the motor vessel *Chester Brook*. The lifeboat escorted both vessels, and on arrival at Padstow at 2.20am on 2 April a doctor provided medical aid to the sick woman. On 22 July 1967 the lifeboat went to the small yacht *Santos*, which was in difficulties on the north side of Harlyn Bay, and escorted her to Padstow harbour. And on 18 October 1967, on what proved to be *Joseph Hiram Chadwick's* last service at Padstow, she went to the motor fishing vessel *Eleanor Anne* of Padstow, which had engine trouble. The fishing vessel's crew of two were taken onto the lifeboat, and the vessel was towed in.

The prototype 44ft Waveney 44-001, an American-designed steel-hulled lifeboat, during a visit to Padstow on 29 May 1964 as part of her evaluation tour round the country. (Grahame Farr, by courtesy of RNLI)

Less than a month after this service, on 16 November 1967, the harbour station was closed and operations were transferred to a new station at Trevose Head, described below. *Joseph Hiram Chadwick* was taken to Falmouth Boat Company for survey and overhaul, having been reallocated to the Galway Bay station in Ireland. She served there for a further eight years, and after a couple of years as a Relief lifeboat was sold out of service in April 1980. She became a private pleasure boat and was renamed *Julia Clare*, being kept on the south coast. In the 1990s she was sold and, under new ownership, was moved to Norfolk and renamed *Forceful*. In 2008, having spent many years at Beccles, a complete restoration was begun by a new owner, who also restored her lifeboat name.

Right: Gordon Elliot was Coxswain from August 1964 to December 1971. (By courtesy of Padstow RNLI)

Far right: George Pinch served as Mechanic from 1961 to 1970

The move to Trevose

A major investment was made by the RNLI at Padstow during the 1960s following serious problems with the silting up of the Doom Bar and the Camel estuary. The problems made launching the lifeboat, which was moored in the Pool outside Padstow Harbour, increasingly difficult, 'seriously interfering with the operational efficiency of the lifeboat station', according to The Lifeboat journal for March 1966. A new home had to be found for the lifeboat where it could be launched at all states of the tide and a site at Trevose Head overlooking Mother Ivey's Bay was proposed. Before making a decision on the viability of building a new station there, however, the RNLI took careful wave recordings over a period of two years at a site. The result showed that a slipway station built at Trevose Head would enable the lifeboat to launch in any weather conditions, although in certain circumstances rehousing may not always be possible immediately and so the decision was taken by the RNLI in 1965 to build a new station.

The Lifeboat journal announced the new development: 'The RNLI has decided to build a new life-boat station at Trevose Head in Cornwall at an approximate cost of £114,600. The work is expected to be completed in about two years.' This was a major investment by the Institution at a time when finances

The 48ft 6in Oakley James and Catherine Macfarlane was built for Padstow in 1967 and was the first lifeboat to operate from the Trevose Head lifeboat house. (By courtesy of Padstow RNLI)

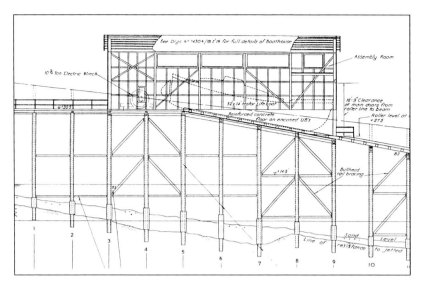

Line drawing of the new lifeboat house and slipway at Trevose Head. The new station consisted of a boathouse 30ft above beach level on the foreshore at the foot of the cliffs, with a slipway 240ft in length.

were somewhat tight, and shows the importance of the station at Padstow. Work began in 1965 with the project undertaken by John Mowlam's subsidiary, E. Thomas & Co Ltd, Falmouth, who had to overcome the awkward geographical situation working at the base of a 120ft cliff down which the materials for the job had to be lowered. The bed rock of slate was covered by sand and shingle to a depth of two to six feet and the steel piles which supported the access gangway, the boathouse and the slipway were placed in holes drilled through the overlaying sand and shingle into the slate below. The lining tubes of the boreholes were left in position below low water and filled with concrete after the piles had been placed in position.

A five-ton derrick with a 150ft crane was erected following the completion of a quarter-of-a-mile long access road, which had to be built across the headland from an adjoining farm track. A short sea wall was also built and a temporary platform erected from which a few piles were sunk and the first part of the steelwork constructed. A travelling gantry was erected on this structure from which the remainder of the piling operations on the 348ft long slipway were carried out, with the slipway having a gradient of one in five and a half. In total, sixty-seven piles were sunk on the project, each measuring eight inches square and grouted a minimum of four foot into twelve-diameter holes bored into solid rock. Because the structural steelwork for the slipway was delivered to the site drilled and ready for erection, accurate positioning of the piles was crucial. As building work progressed, and the slipway extended further into the sea, a transporter bogie was used to carry material and piles to the drilling platform.

Work was carried out twenty-four hours a day on the piling and steel erection, with other operations on a single shift basis included the encasement of piles and transom beams above the low water mark with conventional reinforced concrete, the erection of the galvanised steel slipway, the fitting of the greenheart fendering and the casting of a reinforced concrete deck on the steelwork for the boathouse. Despite the difficult conditions, and the fact that about a month's

The new lifeboat station at Trevose Head under construction. The boathouse was 30ft above beach level on the foreshore at the foot of the cliffs, which at that point are about 100ft high. A new road, a quarter of-a-mile long, was constructed from the Coastguard station to the top of the cliff.

The lifeboat house and slipway at Trevose Head under construction. It was completed in 1967, became operational on 23 October 1967 and was used until 2006. (By courtesy of the RNLI)

working time was lost due to bad weather, the piling and structural steelwork was completed in little over twelve months. The final task was the completion of the boathouse, which was a timber frame structure clad with asbestos 72ft long by 25ft wide in size. The boathouse was approached by cliff stairway and then via a reinforced concrete gangway from the sea wall, while a hoist was installed on the cliff face to make access up and down the steep cliff easier. E. Thomas's contract was worth £104,000 and the site agent was G. E. D. Duff, BSc, the consulting engineers were Lewis and Duvivier, the drilling sub-contractors were Soil Mechanics Ltd, and the steelwork was supplied and fabricated by Slades of Hayle. The work took two years to complete and the new station became operational on 23 October 1967.

As well as a new boathouse, the station was allocated a new 48ft 6in Oakley class self-righting lifeboat. The new boat, named *James and Catherine Macfarlane*, was the second of the class to be built and was completed at the Lymington boatyard of Berthon Boat Company. Costing £61,317, she was funded from the gift of Robert E. Macfarlane, of Glasgow, in memory of his father and mother. She was powered by twin 110hp Gardner 6LX diesel engines, with a two to one reduction gearbox driving twin propellers protected by tunnels, and she had a speed of about nine knots. All the controls were centralised near the coxswain at the wheel, and for the first time a radar set was fitted.

The 48ft 6in Oakley, with a cabin and shelter for the crew and survivors, was a relatively new design which incorporated the self-righting principle developed by the RNLI's Surveyor of Lifeboats, Richard Oakley. The lifeboat, as with the smaller 37ft version developed in the 1950s, had a water ballast tank beneath the engines which filled automatically when the boat entered the sea, and, in the

James and Catherine Macfarlane being launched down the slipway at Trevose Head. The first part of the slipway carried the lifeboat down on rollers for 120ft. The boat then slides down 72ft of the galvanised steel and finally down the 96ft of greenheart keelway. The design was devised so that the boat entered the water at the same speed irrespective of the height of the tide.

event of a capsize, one and a half tons of water was transferred into a righting tank on the port side, which righted the boat. The water passed through three trunks or pipes, in each of which was fitted a valve designed to open when the boat heeled over to an angle of about 110 degrees.

The Padstow boat, the second of the class, was capsized on trials on 23 June 1966 at Portsmouth dockyard, a test which proved that she would right herself in five and seven seconds. Although the hull was a displacement shape, similar to the Liverpool and Barnett lifeboats which had served Padstow previously, in other respects the new lifeboat was a major step forward, being self-righting and carrying more advanced electronic equipment. Throughout her sixteen-year career at Padstow, *James and Catherine Macfarlane* was fitted with more advanced electronic equipment, including better radar and radio communications, during her regular refits. She was placed on station on 19 July 1967 with the operational opening taking place on 23 October 1967.

The officially opening of the new boathouse took place on 19 July 1968 with HRH The Duke of Kent performing the honours. He was deputising for his mother, the late Princess Marina, The Duchess of Kent, President of the RNLI, who had entered a London Hospital. Mr J. C. F. Prideaux-Brune, president of the Padstow station branch, opened the proceedings and expressed regret that Princess Marina had been unable to attend. The two telegrams which she sent to the Padstow ladies' lifeboat guild and the Padstow branch were read. The Duke of Kent, in reading his mother's speech, spoke of the silting up of Padstow harbour which made it necessary to build a new station at Trevose and recalled, too, that the Macfarlane family had also given the lifeboat then stationed at Aith

The 48ft 6in Oakley class James and Catherine Macfarlane being launched down the slipway at Trevose Head for the first time. (RNLI)

in Shetland. Admiral Sir Wilfrid Woods, KCB, DSO, Chairman of the RNLI's Committee of Management, handed over the lifeboat to the branch and she was accepted by A. G. Trembath, honorary secretary. The Assistant Bishop of Truro, the Right Rev W. Q. Lash, dedicated the lifeboat, assisted by the Rev B. B. Clarke, Vicar of Padstow, the Rev W. J. Palmer, Methodist Minister, and the Rev Paul Rea, Roman Catholic Priest of St Mary's Abbey.

The first service by the new lifeboat was undertaken on 21 August 1968 after the motor boat *Spes*, with six people and a dog on board, was reported to be overdue. She had last been sighted one and a half miles north-east of Galland island. *James and Catherine Macfarlane*, which had been launched at 2.30pm because it was the local lifeboat day, slipped her moorings immediately and undertook an extensive search of the area without success. She returned to Padstow at 5.30pm when it was learnt that *Spes* was still missing and her position was now given as the Newland island area. The lifeboat put to sea for a second time at 6pm and after another extensive search found the motor boat nine miles north of Sheppey Point at about 9pm. The motor boat's engine had broken down, so she was taken in tow and brought into Padstow.

James and Catherine Macfarlane served at Padstow for just over sixteen years, during which time she is credited with saving sixty-three lives and was involved in a number of very fine services. Most of her services were routine in nature, and 1969 being one of her busiest years. On 2 May 1969 she was launched during the evening in a moderate south easterly breeze to a small boat firing red flares a mile north of the lifeboat station and found the yacht *Rosemary*, with two people on board, south of Gulland rock with a broken-down engine. She was

The newly-built James and Catherine Macfarlane at St Malo, France, where she was on display for the 10th International Lifeboat Conference from 4 to 9 June 1967. (Grahame Farr, by courtesy of the RNLI)

The scene in Padstow harbour during the naming ceremony of 48ft 6in Oakley James and Catherine Macfarlane on 19 July 1968. She was named by HRH Duke of Kent. (Derek Harvey, by courtesy of Paul Richards)

Padstow lifeboat crew in 1967 with James and Catherine Macfarlane in the new Trevose Head lifeboat house. Left to right: Trevor England, Arthur Permewan, George Pinch (Mechanic), Gordon Elliot (Coxswain), Donnie McBurnie (second coxswain), Norman Pheby, Peter Revely, John Harris and Mr Walker (shore crew). (By courtesy of Padstow RNLI)

investigate a report of red flares. The wind was north-westerly near gale force seven, gusting to force eight, with a very rough, steep, breaking sea over heavy onshore swell. Soon after launching, while on a south-westerly course towards Trevose Head, the lifeboat encountered two particularly heavy seas on the starboard bow. Coxswain Anthony Warnock reduced speed and the next sea, estimated to be 25ft high, broke heavily on the starboard bow, falling onto the almost stationary boat. A considerable weight of water dropped vertically onto

On board James and Catherine Macfarlane in the boathouse in 1967 are Gordon Elliot (Coxswain) at the wheel with Donnie McBurnie (Second Coxswain) standing alongside. Mechanic George Pinch can just be seen on the bench seat. (By courtesy of Padstow RNLI)

the canopy forward of the wheelhouse, smashing the windscreen and damaging the wheelhouse, leaving the coxswain, second coxswain and three crew members injured. Four of them suffered cuts from the broken glass to the head, face and hands, two requiring stitches. The fifth man had damaged ribs, but the other crew members were unhurt.

Coxswain Warnock received a bad cut over his right eye, which temporarily blinded him, and some concussion. He was taken to the after cabin for first aid treatment and Second Coxswain/Assistant Mechanic Trevor England took over. By good judgement and seamanship, he brought the boat back to station at 11.35pm and successfully rehoused her just after midnight on 8 December to land the injured men. Although it was unnecessary for the lifeboat to launch again, Second Coxswain England said that he could have mustered a crew who would have been prepared to take the boat to sea before the repairs were completed, should an urgent call have come, and the honorary secretary commented, 'All the crew have great faith in their lifeboat and were prepared to go to sea again without windscreen or wheelhouse doors'. With the help of Mashford's Yard, Cremyll, and staff from the RNLI Depot, repairs were immediately put in hand and carried out on the slipway. *James and Catherine Macfarlane* was available for service throughout, if an urgent call had come, and was back on full service, with repairs completed, late on the same evening, 8 December. Following this service, a framed certificate inscribed on vellum was presented to Coxswain Warnock, Second Coxswain England, Acting Mechanic A. Prosser, Acting Assistant Mechanic A. May and crew members R. Tummon, A. House and R. Norfolk.

James and Catherine Macfarlane on exercise off the Cornish coast. (By courtesy of Padstow RNLI)

Coxswain Antony Warnock introduces HRH the Duke of Kent to his crew in 1978. Right to left are Second Coxswain Trevor England, Motor Mechanic Eddie Murt, Chris Hughes, Peter Poole, Arthur May, Alf Prosser and Ricky Tummon. (By courtesy of RNLI)

Another outstanding service was undertaken on 17 July 1977 after the 17ft Bermudan sloop *Calcutta Princess* was reported in difficulty a quarter of a mile south-west of Dinas Head. She was losing her sails, had a rope around the propeller of her outboard engine and was drifting towards the Head in rough seas with a man, a woman, and a dog on board. *James and Catherine Macfarlane* was launched at 5.34pm with Coxswain Tony Warnock in command as the lifeboat faced south-westerly strong to near gale force six to seven winds, with visibility about a mile in driving rain.

About eleven minutes after launching, the lifeboat crew sighted the casualty sixty yards from the rocks of Dinas Head, with her bow into the flood with the strong south-westerly wind creating heavy confused sea with waves 15ft to 20ft high. Coxswain Warnock took the lifeboat down the yacht's port side, between the casualty and Dinas Head, and the crew threw a heaving line to the man on board. He appeared exhausted, however, and could not pull the tow rope aboard fast enough, so that it fouled the lifeboat's starboard screw.

Second Coxswain Trevor England then secured the free bight of the tow rope to the guardrail forward of the screw and cut the tow rope free from the after bollard, while the lifeboat came round to starboard, bow to bow with the yacht. With crew members Chris Hughes and Peter Poole, he took down the slack in the heaving line, which the casualty's owner had secured to a cleat on his deck, while Coxswain Warnock put his remaining engine slow astern, in order to pull the yacht clear of danger as quickly as possible. About 30 yards had been gained when a large wave struck the yacht, pulling out the cleat to which the heaving line was secured and jamming the little finger of crew member Chris Hughes between the heaving line and a guardrail stanchion, severing the top third of his finger. At about the same time the end of the tow rope came clear of the lifeboat's propeller. With the yacht drifting clear of Dinas Head but now moving rapidly towards Bull Rock, there was no time to lose.

By the time the lifeboat had turned 360 degrees to port, the casualty was no more than 25ft from Bull Rock. Nevertheless, Coxswain Warnock took the lifeboat between the rock and the yacht, holding her clear while Second Coxswain England dropped the tow rope on to her deck. With both boats ranging up to 20ft the successful passing of the tow rope was a difficult feat. Chris Hughes had been obliged to sit in the wheelhouse because of faintness after the loss of the portion of his finger. Nevertheless, he not only declined help so that operations on deck would not be jeopardised, but also manned the VHF so that Coxswain

Anthony Warnock served as Coxswain from January 1972 to August 1978. (By courtesy of the RNLI)

Warnock could concentrate on manoeuvring the lifeboat. The seas around The Bull were highly confused and only the backwash of the 20ft waves kept the lifeboat a boathook's length from the rock face. It was impossible to board the yacht, but the owner eventually managed to secure the tow rope around his mast. Coxswain Warnock then went astern and towed the sloop to safety and calmer water about a quarter of a mile to the south west, where the occupants were taken on board the lifeboat.

James and Catherine Macfarlane seen from the air in 1971, with her superstructure painted white. (By courtesy of Padstow RNLI)

James and
Catherine
Macfarlane
approaching the
slipway at Trevose
Head prior to
being recovered.
(By courtesy of
the RNLI)

It was now 6.10pm and the lifeboat set course for her station with *Calcutta Princess* in tow, while First Aider Alf Prosser rendered emergency treatment to the injured Chris Hughes and First Aider Arthur May treated the yacht's crew for hypothermia and shock. A helicopter from HMS *Hermes* arrived to lift off the survivors and the injured lifeboatman for medical treatment aboard the carrier, but the transfer was deferred until the survivors had been landed at the slipway at 7pm. The casualties were then immediately airlifted to *Hermes*, thus reaching hospital facilities much more rapidly than they would have done by the alternative of ambulance to Truro. The lifeboat then towed the yacht into Padstow harbour and secured her alongside the quay and the lifeboat then returned to station, being rehoused by 8.45pm. For this service the silver medal for gallantry was awarded to Coxswain Warnock and Second Coxswain/ Assistant Mechanic England. The Thanks of the Institution inscribed on Vellum was accorded to crew members Chris Hughes, Arthur May, Alfred Prosser, Peter Poole and Richard Tummon.

James and Catherine Macfarlane faced further heavy seas on Christmas Eve, 24 December 1977, with her crew at sea for a long and difficult search. Together with the St Ives and Clovelly lifeboats, they were involved in a prolonged search in a south-westerly storm after the Danish coaster *Lady Kamilla*, with a crew of nine, foundered off Trevose Head. In addition to the three lifeboats, HMS *Sherington*, Nimrod aircraft, Wessex and Sea King helicopters and various merchant vessels which were in the vicinity also took part. *Lady Kamilla*, which had originally reported taking water in her hatches, foundered and sank before help arrived. The crew abandoned ship and two survivors were picked up from a liferaft by helicopter. No other survivors were found, although wreckage identified as coming from *Lady Kamilla* was sighted. *James and Catherine Macfarlane* was at sea searching for almost fifteen hours, as was the Clovelly lifeboat *City of Bristol*; St Ives lifeboat, the 37ft Oakley *Frank Penfold Marshall*, suffered damage when she was hit by an exceptionally large sea, after six hours of involvement in the search.

Padstow lifeboat launched at just after midnight with eight crew aboard, Coxswain Tony Warnock taking an extra crew member because of the severe weather, and headed for the position of the casualty. She arrived at the search area at 3.20am and started a box search in very difficult conditions. At 2.30pm it was reported that two survivors had been picked up from a liferaft by a helicopter in a position about twenty miles to the north. As the lifeboat could not reach this new search area before dark she was recalled and returned to station at 3.12pm to be rehoused. The St Ives lifeboat had faced the most testing conditions and her Coxswain, Thomas Cocking, and crew had survived a knockdown, after which Coxswain Cocking was awarded the silver medal for gallantry and the Thanks of the Institution inscribed on Vellum was accorded to Second Coxswain John Perkin, Mechanic Philip Penberthy, Assistant Mechanic David Smith, Emergency Mechanic John Thomas, Signalman Eric Ward and Radio Operator

Crew in front of James and Catherine Macfarlane are, left to right, Pat Rabey (head launcher), Eddy Murt (Mechanic), Ian Macer, Edward Hicks, Ricky Tummon (Second Coxswain), Bill Tippett, Trevor England (Coxswain), Robert Norfolk, Chris Hughes and Fred Norfolk. (By courtesy of Padstow RNLI)

one fender was lost overboard and Coxswain England decided to retrieve it in order to see if it would be possible to rescue survivors from the water.

Although the helicopters could not communicate with the casualty, the lifeboat id establish contact with *Skopelos Sky* and Coxswain England asked the master if he could anchor, receiving the reply that it was too rough to send a man on to the fo'c'sle. Three men were lifted off by the helicopter, but the helicopter's winchman hit the freighter's superstructure three times and the pilot suggested the lifeboat go in for the remainder. The casualty steamed head to sea and the survivors were gathered aft, but the height of decks was such that it depended on the arrival of the right sea at the appropriate moment to carry the lifeboat high enough to get the men off. The lifeboat was ranging

James and Catherine Macfarlane going to the aid of the freighter Skopelos Sky. (By courtesy of Padstow RNLI)

The freighter Skopelos Sky aground and breaking up on the rocks below Doyden Point after the dramatic rescue by the Padstow lifeboat. (By courtesy of Padstow RNLI)

between the level of the casualty's propeller boss and her main deck. Coxswain England used all his very considerable boat-handing skill and the full power of his engines during the difficult operation, but the lifeboat's forward fairlead was badly damaged when *Skopelos Sky* rolled heavily on to the lifeboat at one point. After five alongside attempts, during which one man threw his suitcase down on to the lifeboat, the freighter's crew waved the lifeboat away indicating that they would only abandon ship by helicopter. Throughout the five attempts to get alongside Second Coxswain Tummon and his deck party were on the foredeck of the lifeboat ready to receive the survivors.

Coxswain England had by now concluded that rescue by lifeboat was impossible, except perhaps from the sea itself, and so he asked the helicopter to try again. The lifeboat then stood by the casualty's stern while seven more men were lifted. It was just after 11am and the helicopter asked the lifeboat to remain standing by until further notice. *Skopelos Sky* then began steaming east-west in a figure-of-eight pattern across Portquin Bay at five knots, with the wind and sea mainly on alternate beams, still with her starboard list due to the shift of cargo. At 2pm the wind was still gusting to force twelve and the state of the sea in Portquin Bay was awesome. People watching from the 200ft cliffs at Doyden Point were losing sight of the lifeboat completely for seconds at a time, although she was no more than a quarter of a mile off shore. Coxswain England afterwards said he felt like 'an insect in a ploughed field', but the lifeboat kept constant station on the casualty's quarter, taking every possible advantage of whatever lee the freighter herself afforded but being dangerously exposed every time *Skopelos Sky* reversed her course. Then it was only the most skilful handling by the coxswain in meeting the worst of the waves which was preventing a capsize.

Arrangements were being made for Clovelly's 71ft Clyde class lifeboat *City of Bristol* to take over from Padstow lifeboat at dusk, with Padstow relieving again in the morning. Clovelly lifeboat had to be diverted to answer another call, however, and Coxswain England said he would be willing to remain with *Skopelos Sky* all night if necessary. By 3pm it was apparent that it would be dark before long and helicopter rescue might be impossible. Coxswain England advised the master of the casualty to steam to seaward and drop both anchors and all the cable he had in an attempt to save the ship, but the master was unwilling to take this action because of the heavy seas being shipped over the fo'c'sle.

As the situation deteriorated, a helicopter lift could no longer be delayed and helicopter Rescue 21 asked the lifeboat to inform the casualty that the remaining crew should come off now. At about 4pm the master said he would head into wind to drop anchor and would be ready to be lifted off in about fifteen minutes. He asked the lifeboat to stand close by while he sent a man forward to let go the anchor in case the man should be washed overboard. The lifeboat came in as close as possible to the freighter's side and the anchor was dropped at about 4.20pm, and within fifteen minutes Rescue 21 had lifted off three more, by when it was dark. The master and one oiler were still on board and they shut down *Skopelos Sky's* engines and switched off all her lights as she lay with her bows to the south-west and began drifting in with the lifeboat still between her and the shore. By 5pm only the master remained to be lifted. Rescue 21 had departed and a Sea King, Rescue 90, using her searchlight, was trying to lift the master from the after end of the ship.

At 5.10pm Coxswain England reported that he estimated the casualty would be ashore in about fifteen minutes. Soon afterwards the people on the cliffs lost sight of the lifeboat as she disappeared under the headland over which spray was still flying. Five minutes later the coxswain reported that he was now pulling out from between the casualty and the shore. The Sea King was still trying to rescue the last man as *Skopelos Sky* grounded below Doyden Point at 5.23pm. Then he

James and Catherine Macfarlane on service to the yacht Calcutta Princess. (By courtesy of Padstow RNLI)

James and Catherine Macfarlane towing the local fishing vessel Lamorna into Newquay on 26 January 1982. The vessel ran into difficulties when a rope got wrapped round her propeller about three quarters of a mile off Newquay Head in deteriorating weather. (B.S. White, by courtesy of the RNLI)

was lifted clear and seconds later the entire freighter was obliterated in spray as she was hit by an enormous breaker. As the spray cleared, what had been a list to starboard, that is to seaward, had been transformed into a forty-five degrees list to port, hard among the rocks.

With the tide now at half ebb, it would be eight hours before it would be possible to enter Padstow. The crew were already suffering from their long ordeal with the sea and so Coxswain England decided to try to rehouse. There was a certain amount of shelter at the foot of the slipway and the wind had moderated to gale force eight to strong gale force nine by the time the lifeboat arrived at Trevose Head at 6.10pm, but there was still a heavy run on the boathouse slipway. Coxswain England found the keelway on his first attempt but the lifeboat ranged 30ft up and down the slipway and the haul-up span was damaged by the keel. The lifeboat was then held clear on her engines and breasting ropes for thirty minutes while the spare span was fitted and the winch wire re-flaked by the launchers, who were at times being submerged up to their necks. Coxswain England put her back on the slipway, again at the first attempt and, though ranging and thumping very hard, she was hauled clear at 7pm. No damage had been sustained except that to her bow, received when she was alongside the casualty, and she was reported ready for service an hour later.

For this truly outstanding service a bar to his silver medal was awarded to Coxswain England and the Thanks of the Institution on Vellum were accorded to Second Coxswain/Assistant Mechanic Richard Tummon, Mechanic Horace Murt, Emergency Mechanics Arthur May and Peter Poole and crew members Sidney Porter, Allan Tarby and Edward Hicks. The Thanks on Vellum were also accorded to each of the slipway helpers: head launcher Patrick Rabey, shore attendant John Thomas, assistant winchman William Tucker and shore helpers Ian Macer, Timothy Lloyd, Ian Kendall, Stewart Porter and Frederick Norfolk. A vellum service certificate was presented to winchman Ernest Bennett.

One onlooker, Air Commodore A.E. Clouston, RAF (Retd), later wrote to Coxswain England to congratulate him and his crew. In his letter he said:

James and Catherine Macfarlane at the foot of the slipway at the start of the recovery procedure. (By courtesy of Padstow RNLI)

'Local old timers and seafarers agree the storm was the worst in living memory. From my house I overlook Constantine Bay and Trevose Head and I have never seen such seas. When the radio announced a ship was in distress and the Padstow lifeboat had been called out, considering the hurricane conditions prevailing I gave you small chance of surviving. The fact you and your crew launched, gave assistance and returned safely speaks volumes for your capability as seamen. This was the most outstanding act of unselfish courage and seamanship that I have known in my lifetime ... All due credit to the excellent work of your shore-based launching and recovery crew who made your trip possible.'

Coxswain Trevor England in the wheelhouse of James and Catherine Macfarlane. (By courtesy of Padstow RNLI)

During 1980 the relief lifeboat *Gertrude* again returned to Padstow, while *James and Catherine Macfarlane* went to Falmouth Boat Co for survey. *Gertrude* completed several routine services, including twice landing injured men from fishing vessels, during her two months on station. *James and Catherine Macfarlane* returned on 31 May 1980 and a few months later was involved in another very fine service. On 16 October 1980 the fishing vessel *Girl Christian* was reported to be in difficulties four miles north

The lifeboat crew in the 1970s, left to right: Ernie Bennett, Pat Rabey Ian Macer, Ian Kendall, Trevor England, Tony Warnock (Coxswain), Eddy Murt (Mechanic), Arthur May, R. Tummon, Alf Prosser, Steven Thomas, Alan House, Peter Poole and Harry Lobb (Hon Secretary). (By courtesy of Padstow RNLI)

of Trevose Head so *James and Catherine Macfarlane* launched at 2.18am under the command of Coxswain Trevor England into force six winds and rough seas. *Girl Christian*, with two men on board, was in tow of another fishing vessel, *Minehead Angler*, with three on board and the two boats were heading south. The lifeboat reached them at 2.53pm and a few minutes later reported that she would escort them to Newquay. By 3.30am the north-easterly wind was gusting to near gale force seven, and half an hour later *Girl Christian* and *Minehead Angler* dropped anchor in the shelter of Porth Island to await the tide before entering Newquay. As both fishing boats were now suffering engine trouble, and because of the deteriorating weather, it was decided that the lifeboat should stand by until they had entered harbour.

At 7.17am the lifeboat weighed anchor and made for Newquay to assess the conditions, but with seas breaking heavily at the harbour entrance she advised the fishing boats to remain at anchor. At 8.08am the lifeboat entered Newquay and at 8.40am, with the sea quietening, it was agreed that the two fishing boats should weigh anchor and enter harbour. They came in one at a time as *Girl Christian* had managed to get her engine going and *Minehead Angler* had engine trouble of her own. Padstow lifeboat escorted the boats in, and by 9.12am both were safely moored alongside the quay. The lifeboat crew were given breakfast at Newquay and set out on the return passage to Padstow soon after 10am. On reaching station, recovery was difficult, but *James and Catherine Macfarlane* was rehoused at 12.30pm. For this service a letter signed by Cdr Bruce Cairns, chief of operations, expressing appreciation to Coxswain Trevor England and his crew was sent to Lt Cdr J.W. Hamilton, Padstow station honorary secretary.

What proved to be the final service by *James and Catherine Macfarlane* during her time at Padstow was undertaken 26 August 1983 when she went to Port Isaac to assist the local inshore lifeboat, which was stranded in surf on the northern side of Trebarwith Strand. A line was fired very accurately to the ILB, which was recovered and taken to Port Isaac. The crew for this service were Coxswain Trevor England, Second Coxswain R. Tummon, E. Murt, A. May, Allan Tarby, T. Lloyd, W. Tippett, B. Murt, W. Lobb and W. Phillips.

On 10 September 1983 *James and Catherine Macfarlane* left the station to go for refit at Falmouth Boat Company's yard, and the former St Mary's lifeboat *Guy and Clare Hunter* arrived on relief duty. She launched seven times and saved three lives during her time at the station. While James and Catherine Macfarlane was away, a new 47ft Tyne class lifeboat was allocated to Padstow and, as a result, the Oakley was reallocated to The Lizard, being readied for her new station at the boatyard, which she left in July 1984 to go straight to The Lizard. With the Oakley going to The Lizard, the 52ft Barnett *The Duke of Cornwall (Civil Service No.33)*, which had served at The Lizard but now been replaced, was sent to Padstow as a temporary measure until the arrival of the new Tyne. The Barnett arrived at Padstow on 31 July 1984, releasing *Guy and Clare Hunter* for service elsewhere, and she stayed until the new 47ft Tyne was ready. *The Duke of Cornwall* remained as Padstow lifeboat until being replaced in late December 1984, and she left the station on 4 January 1985 for five more years of service serving in the RNLI's relief fleet.

During her time on station, *The Duke of Cornwall* undertook a notable service in heavy weather during the night of 21 to 22 October 1984 after the yacht Talahinna got into difficulty with engine and rigging failure ten miles north east of Trevose Head. Deputy Coxswain Christopher Hughes was in command when *The Duke of Cornwall* launched at 8.53pm. On clearing the slipway, the lifeboat turned to port and met the full force of the rough seas whipped up by the south-westerly force seven gale, gusting to force eight at times, while heavy rain reduced visibility. At 9.05pm the German ship *Wega* reported seeing a

James and Catherine Macfarlane inside the lifeboat house at Trevose Head. (By courtesy of Padstow RNLI)

distress flare from the casualty and, at the acting coxswain's request, the German coaster switched on her deck lights and fired a parachute flare, which could be seen from the lifeboat. At 10.34pm the lifeboat fired a parachute flare and the crew saw the yacht lying beam on to the wind and sea, rolling heavily, with seas occasionally breaking over her. Acting Coxswain Hughes approached the lee side of the yacht and established that six people were on board and they wanted to be taken in tow.

Wega provided a lee for the two boats as the lifeboat passed a heaving line across and the tow began at 10.48pm. A speed of three knots was maintained, but as the yacht sheered and snatched at the line the tow was stopped and two heavy fenders were attached to the mid-point, after which towing was resumed and speed was increased to four to five knots. Just after 1am on 22 October,

James and Catherine Macfarlane stripped down during a routine overhaul at Mashfords yard. (By courtesy of Padstow RNLI)

with the boats under the slight lee of Stepper Point, speed was eased while the tow line was shortened, and half an hour later Acting Coxswain Hughes safely negotiated the bar and entered Padstow harbour, where the yacht was secured alongside. The lifeboat was rehoused, refuelled and ready once again for service at 4am on 22 October. Following this service a letter, signed by RNLI Director Rear Admiral W. J. Graham, was sent to Deputy Coxswain Hughes expressing appreciation of his seamanship and boat handling. Letters of thanks were also sent to the district controller of Falmouth Coastguard and to the owners of the coaster *Wega* for the part her captain played in the service.

After service at Padstow, James and Catherine Macfarlane served at The Lizard for three years and in 1988 was loaned for display at the Lands End complex as a visitor attraction. In 2016 she was sold to a private buyer for restoration. (Nicholas Leach)

James Burrough

During the 1960s significant developments took place in offshore lifeboat design, all intended to meet changing demands on the lifeboat service and the need for lifeboats to reach casualties more quickly. Faster offshore lifeboats were needed and the first fast RNLI lifeboat, the Waveney class, was based on a United States Coast Guard (USCG) design for a 44ft steel-hulled rescue boat. The RNLI purchased one of these boats from the USCG in 1963 and took it on a tour of lifeboat stations in Britain and Ireland, which included a visit to Padstow, to assess its suitability and ascertain crew opinions. It was a radical departure from the traditional designs then used by the RNLI, but crews were very positive about the boat and it was soon accepted into service. The Waveney and the larger 52ft Arun, introduced soon afterwards, were designed for operations from an afloat berth, so stations where slipway or carriage launching was employed needed other designs. Therefore, in the late 1970s the RNLI began designing a fast lifeboat type to be launched from a slipway to replace the Watson and Barnett type lifeboats and, as at Padstow, the 48ft 6in Oakley and Solent types. Slipway launching required a hull which protects the propellers and rudders, while the hull itself has to be sufficiently strong to withstand the stresses of being hauled up a slipway.

The basic lines plan for the hull of the 'fast slipway boat' (FSB), as it was originally known, was provided by the National Maritime Institute and featured a semi-planing hull, constructed from steel, with a shallow draught, long straight keel and flared bow above the waterline. Protection for the propellers was given

The prototype 47ft Tyne City of London on trials. Completed in 1981, after being used for trials she served at Selsey for twenty-three years. (By courtesy of the RNLI)

by partial tunnels, substantial bilge keels, and a straight wide keel ending in a
hauling shoe for winching the boat back into its house, all necessary for slipway
launching. The wheelhouse had a low profile to fit into existing boathouses,
with a flying bridge amidships and a separate cabin aft of the upper steering
position. The hull shape of the new design enabled a top speed of approximately
eighteen knots to be achieved by the twin propellers, which were driven by two
425hp General Motors 6V-92-TI diesel engines. The two main tanks carried 510
gallons of diesel between them, with a reserve tank of 102 gallons, giving a range
at full speed of 238 nautical miles.

The design was given the class name Tyne in line with the RNLI's policy
of using names of rivers for lifeboat classes and the prototype, ON-1074, was
taken on a tour of the country during 1982 under the command of District
Inspector Tom Nutman and Staff Coxswain A. Hunter. Soon after ON-1074 had
ended her tour, the RNLI ordered a further four Tynes from the Fairey Marine
boatyard at Cowes and these was allocated to Padstow, Holyhead, The Mumbles
and Cromer. Meanwhile, the prototype boat was named *City of London* and in
November 1983 went on station at Selsey, while the second prototype, ON-1075,
was allocated to the Relief Fleet and named *Sam and Joan Woods*.

The Padstow boat, the third Tyne with the operational number 47-003, was
funded by Miss H.B. 'Mickie' Allen, of Clandon, near Guildford, cost £451,906,
and was named James Burrough in memory of the donor's great grandfather.
She was completed in May 1984 and went on an extensive series of trials for the
rest of the year. However, she had a number of problems during her forty-hour

trial, so most of the summer was taken with proving trials to ensure the new boat was suitable for service. She complete thirty hours without breaking down to prove her reliability, and was then accepted into service. During these trials, she undertook her first service, on 8 November 1984 while she was working out of Poole, assisting the Medina lifeboat ON-1072 which had engine problems and so was towed back to the RNLI Depot by 47-003.

The Padstow crew spent a week training on their new boat at Poole during mid-December 1984, with the boat being brought to her new station afterwards. The passage to Cornwall took James Burrough and her crew via Weymouth, Guernsey, Plymouth and Newlyn, and she arrived at Padstow on 21 December. Further crew training took place between Christmas and New Year, when the new boat was taken to Lundy among various other places. Once this training had been completed, she was officially placed on station on 28 December. Her

James Burrough
arrives at Padstow
for the first time,
December 1984.
Her delivery
crew comprised
Coxswain Trevor
England, Second
Coxswain Ricky
Tummon, Mechanic
Eddie Murt and
crew Alan Tarby,
Bernard Murt, Tim
Lloyd and Edward
Hicks. Inspector
Les Vipond was
in charge during
the passage.
(By courtesy of
Padstow RNLI)

first service at Padstow was on 20 February 1985 when she launched to the
fifteen-ton fishing vessel *Lady Joanna*, which was taking in water about five miles
west of Newquay. The lifeboat stood by while the vessel made her own way
back to Newquay.

The naming ceremony of the new lifeboat took place on 15 April 1985 with
crowds of well-wishers lining the edge of Padstow's inner harbour for the event.
The boat was brought round from Trevose Head and, dressed overall looked
magnificent at her moorings a few feet from the North Quay where 600 guests
were seated. At 3pm the platform party arrived, led by a Deputy Lieutenant of
the county, Vice-Admiral Sir James Jungius, representing the Lord Lieutenant.
Mr Prideaux Brune, the station branch president, opened the proceedings and
paid tribute to Miss H. B. 'Mickie' Allen, the donor.

Miss Allen formally handed the lifeboat to the Duke of Atholl, chairman of
the RNLI, who also paid tribute to Miss Allen's generosity before presenting
the lifeboat to the honorary secretary, Trevor Ramsden. Les Vipond, divisional
inspector of lifeboats for the south west, gave a brief description of the design
and development of the Tyne class and particularly *James Burrough*, which was
only the second of her class to be placed on station. A short service of dedication
followed, led by the Bishop of Truro, the Right Reverend Peter Mumford, and
assisted by the Prior of Bodmin, the Very Reverend Henry Miller, the Methodist
Minister, the Rev Peter Grose, and the station chaplain, the Rev Martin Boxall.
Mr Brad Trethewey, chairman of the branch and also Mayor of Padstow, then
invited Miss Allen to name James Burrough, which she did before boarding

the lifeboat with Admiral Jungius, the Duke of Atholl, and other guests to meet Coxswain Trevor England and his crew for a short trip around the Camel estuary.

On 2 August 1985 *James Burrough* performed two services, launching in the early house to the trawler *Jean Marc*, which was thirty miles west of Trevose. She launched at 3.23am, with a doctor on board to tend to an injured man, and was alongside the casualty in fifty-seven minutes. The injured man was treated and taken on board the lifeboat. While returning to station, and in deteriorating conditions, the lifeboat was diverted to assist the yacht *Seagoe*, which was in difficulty in the worsening conditions. The yacht, which had lost her sails and was taking on water, was taken in tow at 11.14pm and, at slow speed. The vessels headed towards Padstow, but the yacht was sinking, so the tow rope was cut and

James Burrough shows a good turn of speed off the boathouse at Trevose Head. (By courtesy of Padstow RNLI)

James Burrough was the third Tyne class lifeboat to be built out of forty boats completed by the RNLI during the 1980s. She is pictured in the Camel Estuary heading for the harbour.

The lifeboat crew in 1989, from left to right, back to front: Peter Poole, Mick Walker, Peter Rojano, David Bolton, Robert Norfolk, Steve Hughes, Neil Harding, Peter Lobb, Richard Pitman, Paul Masters, Tim Norfolk, Bernard Murt, Mike England, Jason Nicholas, Tim Lloyd, Edward Hicks, Bill Tippett, Alan Tarby (Second Coxswain), John Alldridge (Mech) and Trevor England (Coxswain).

the lifeboat was turned to recover her crew of six from the water. With great skill and seamanship, the lifeboat crew recovered the survivors from the water within six minutes, despite them being dispersed in the water. Crew member Bernard Murt had to enter the water at one stage to assist one of the survivors aboard the lifeboat, which returned to station with the master being treated for shock and exposure. He was subsequently taken to hospital, while the other five survivors were given warm drinks in the boathouse once the lifeboat had been recovered.

On the night of 12 January 1987 *James Burrough* undertook another challenging service. She launched to the 445-ton cargo vessel *Mare*, of Honduras, which was on passage from Rotterdam to Dundalk with a cargo of iron ore and had got into difficulties when her load shifted and she developed a twenty to thirty degree list, twenty-eight miles west north-west of Trevose Head. The skipper of the vessel was concerned about the vessel's situation in the heavy seas and force eight winds, and requested assistance. On arrival alongside the casualty just after 9pm, the lifeboat found the Leander class frigate HMS *Cleopatra* and a helicopter from RNAS Culdrose standing by the stricken ship. *James Burrough* escorted the casualty to Padstow, with HMS *Cleopatra* providing a lee until reaching the shelter of land. The helicopter was released at 9.12pm and, as the vessels approached Padstow at 2.08am on 13 January, HMS *Cleopatra* also left. Mare was safely escorted into Padstow Harbour and the lifeboat, unable to rehouse because of ice on the slipway, moored in the harbour. During this eleven-hour service in a full gale and temperatures well below freezing, ice had formed on the lifeboat's deck and the crew working outside had their clothing frozen. A letter of appreciation from the director of the RNLI, Rear Admiral W. J. Graham, was sent to Coxswain Trevor England and his crew, congratulating them for their efforts over a long period in near Arctic conditions during this difficult service, taking them to the edge of their own physical endurance.

Almost exactly a year later, on 10 January 1988, *James Burrough* launched to the fishing boat *Laura Jane*, which was in difficulty a quarter of a mile off Towan Head in moderate to rough seas, and an intensive search was undertaken for

a missing person. A body found just after 8pm was taken ashore by Newquay inshore lifeboat. Two helicopters, five local fishing vessels, as well as Newquay and Padstow lifeboats were involved in the search, and although much debris was found, no survivors were picked up from the casualty. The wreckage was landed at Newquay harbour, and *James Burrough* then returned to station after the search had been called off at 10.45pm. The following day the lifeboat launch again to continue the search at first light, together with the helicopter and Newquay ILB. The lifeboats worked together in search patterns for four hours, after which the search was called off with 'no sign of missing fishermen', although further wreckage was recovered.

Between 3 May and 24 September 1988 the relief lifeboat *Sam and Joan Woods*, the second Tyne to be built, was on duty while *James Burrough* went to Falmouth Boat Co for repairs and maintenance work to be undertaken. The relief boat undertook eleven services including one on 22 July 1988 to the Port Isaac inshore lifeboat D-366, which capsized south of Penhallick Point. The ILB had been righted by its crew by the time the Padstow lifeboat reached the scene, so the ILB was escorted back to Port Isaac. *Sam and Joan Woods* carried out a number of other routine services, the last of which involved saving two sailboarders on 24 September 1988.

James Burrough returned from the boatyard on 2 October 1988, and on 12 March 1989 she and her crew were involved in a very difficult service for which they received a letter from the RNLI chairman. The lifeboat launched to the Panamanian-registered ship *Secil Japan*, which had issued a Mayday seventeen miles north-west of Trevose Head after her cargo shifted making her list twenty degree. James Burrough put out into south-westerly force eight winds and

47ft Tyne James Burrough served at Padstow from December 1984 until July 2006, during which time she is credited with launching 293 times on service and saving ninety-seven lives.

rough seas, taking fifteen minutes to clear Trevose Head in the severe conditions. A helicopter from RNAS Culdrose found the casualty seven miles off St Agnes Head and the St Ives lifeboat *Frank Penfold Marshall* was also launched.

The pilot of the helicopter had been advising the captain of Secil Japan to keep in deep water, but the captain continued to head towards the coast and eventually dropped both anchors and shut down the main engine. He then asked that his crew be evacuated and a second helicopter was scrambled. The St Ives coxswain manoeuvred his lifeboat ahead of the casualty, anchored and started veering down, but such large seas were encountered that he had to recover his anchor. Padstow lifeboat arrived and also anchored, intending to fire a rocket line and rig the breeches buoy. However as the coxswain started to veer down a helicopter began winching the survivors off and so *James Burrough* also recovered her anchor. Both coxswains decided to stand by while the helicopters winched the crew off, and four crew were lifted off before the winching had to stop.

By 11pm the wind had increased to force eight to nine, gusting to force ten from the north-west. Very rough seas were breaking over the casualty, which was taking the ground astern in the troughs, and the remaining twelve survivors refused to leave the shelter of the wheelhouse. At 11.15pm both of *Secil Japan's* anchor cables parted, and her bow swung to port, putting her starboard side to the sea, and a few minutes later she lost all power and was plunged into darkness. The deck cargo of timber shifted further and was eventually washed away, while the derricks broke free and swung with the movement of the ship. Just before 2am the ship became more stable as low water approached and the helicopter managed to put a crew man on board the casualty. Winching started again but the first man to be winched raised his arms as he neared the helicopter door and slipped from the strop, being lost after he plunged 180ft into the surf. The remaining eleven men were winched into the helicopter by 2.17am, thirty minutes before low water.

Crew on board James Burrough, from left to right, Eddie Murt (Mechanic), Chris Hughes, Trevor England (Coxswain), Bill Tippett and Arthur May. (By courtesy of Padstow RNLI)

Both lifeboats were released and headed for their respective stations. *James Burrough* returned at approximately eight knots, encountering rough seas on the way while St Ives lifeboat took two very heavy seas which poured water into the radar, MF and VHF DF, all of which stopped working. She beached at her station at 3.10am, while *James Burrough* was held off the slipway until daybreak, when she recovered. Due to the extreme weather during this long service both lifeboats suffered damage in the heavy seas, with stanchions bent and control panels, radar displays and radio equipment filled with water. In his report, Divisional Inspector South West John Unwin said that the service could easily have turned into a disaster if either coxswain had not conducted himself in such a cool professional manner. Both coxswains were aware that if they had veered down on the casualty's port side, and the ship had swung into the rocks and cliff, they would have been trapped. 'I commend both crews for their perseverance in getting the anchors on board and retrieving all the anchor cable,' he said, 'and they carried out their duties in a manner that was a credit to the RNLI.'

On 10 July 1991 *James Burrough* and her crew completed another fine service, launching in the early hours to go to the 6oft Weymouth crabber *Kael Coz*, which had gone aground under cliffs at Rumps Point. Fifty feet either way and her bottom would have been ripped out on the underwater rocks. As it was, she was hard and fast, broadside on and rolling heavily with the Atlantic swell. The

Relief 47ft Tyne *Sam and Joan Woods*, the second of the class to be built, approaching the slipway at Trevose Head prior to being recovered after a publicity launch, August 1988. She was on duty at Padstow from March to October 1988 while *James Burrough* went to Falmouth Boat Company for modifications and alterations. (Nicholas Leach)

lifeboat had to go straight in and out again, as there was no other option. The manoeuvre was particularly dangerous, not least because of the heavy swell at the base of the cliffs and the rolling of the casualty, which was later abandoned as a total wreck. Coxswain Trevor England successfully achieved the manoeuvre after four attempts, with the four crew jumping aboard the lifeboat. One of them had his finger tip crushed as he did so, and he had to be treated by the lifeboat crew. After arriving safely at Padstow Harbour, an ambulance took the injured man to hospital. In a letter from the RNLI's chief of operations to the lifeboat crew, they were praised for a service which 'was carried out in dangerous conditions', and which 'called upon each of the crew's individual skills as lifeboatmen'.

On 21 September 1991 *James Burrough* was involved in assisting the crabber *Pearn Pride,* which she was sinking about six miles off Tintagel when water flooded her engine room. Attempts by skipper Tony Conium and his crew to stem the leak failed and *James Burrough* launched at 9am to go to her aid. A helicopter from RNAS Culdrose was also called out, and the trawler *Belle Anne,* which was in the vicinity, joined the rescue operation and took off two of the crabber's crew while efforts were made to pump her out. When his vessel began to roll over, the skipper stepped off and straight aboard *Belle Anne.* The three rescued men were transferred to the lifeboat and landed at the lifeboat station.

In November 1992 Padstow lifeboat crew was involved in two incidents which both ended in tragedy. At about 7.30pm on 22 November 1992 a 14ft fishing punt with two men onboard left Padstow Harbour to fish in the estuary. When they failed to return home at 8.30am the following morning the alarm was raised. *James Burrough* was launched immediately and a search was started, with the Appledore lifeboat *George Gibson* and helicopters from RAF Chivenor and RNAS Culdrose assisting, and Coastguard Cliff Rescue teams from Bude, Tintagel, Port Isaac and St Merryn also involved. Wreckage from the punt was found four miles north-west of Tintagel Head indicating that the punt sank on the Doom Bar. The search was called off at 4pm with no bodies having been found. A few days later the body of Arnold Murt, one of those on the punt, was found near Bude, and the body of the other occupant, Neil Harding, was found at Polzeath Bay. Neil had been on the Padstow crew for ten years.

The second tragedy happened a week later, on 29 November, after the fishing boat *Peganina* left Padstow at to collect crab pots during the morning. She was last seen rounding Stepper Point, crewed by Paul Masters, acting

2nd coxswain of the lifeboat, his cousin David Masters and Peter Hope, who also a member of the lifeboat crew. *Peganina* was expected to arrive back in Padstow at 2.30pm, but when she had not returned by 6pm the lifeboat was launched and began an extensive search for the fishing boat. Lifeboats from St Ives and Appledore, helicopters from RAF Chivenor and RNAS Culdrose and nine large fishing boats from Padstow also joined the search with *James Burrough* acting as on-scene co-ordinator. The first wreckage was sighted the next morning when a wheelhouse door was found, with the St Ives lifeboat finding a mass of wreckage a mile off Stepper Point soon afterwards. The RNAS helicopter's diver found *Peganina* in 79ft of water, but there was no explanation as to why *Peganina*. Peter Hope's body was found a week later, washed ashore near Bude. Paul Masters' body was picked up by Padstow lifeboat on Christmas Eve, but David Masters' body was never found. These incidents affected the people of Padstow for many years, and an appeal was made to raise funds for relatives of those lost.

Crew of James Burrough for her last launch with Trevor England as Coxswain, 24 July 1993. With Trevor (centre) are, left to right, John Alldridge (Mechanic), Alan Tarby (new Coxswain), Michael England (Second Mechanic) and Edward Hicks (new Second Coxswain). (By courtesy of Padstow RNLI)

James Burrough shows a good turn of speed. (By courtesy of Padstow RNLI)

Between October 1991 and January 1992, and then again from March to July 1993, the relief lifeboat *Mariner's Friend* was on duty at the station while *James Burrough* went to boatyards at Falmouth and Appledore for repairs and maintenance work. During her second stint at the station, *Mariner's Friend* was involved in a service which proved to be the last for Coxswain Trevor England. The lifeboat launched to the former minesweeper *Margherita*, which was taking in water five miles north-east of Padstow. A helicopter took a pump to the casualty, which was escorted back to Padstow by *Mariner's Friend* and assisted into the inner harbour. Crewing the lifeboat with Coxswain England were, among others, his replacement Alan Tarby as well as his son, Mike England, who was later appointed the station's full-time mechanic. A retirement party was held for Trevor on 24 July 1993 at the Metropole, with the Coxswain retiring after thirty-six years of service on the lifeboat having followed in the footsteps of his father and grandfather. On 27 August 1993 Alan Tarby performed his first service as Coxswain during the station's annual lifeboat day when a 16ft punt had engine failure by Gulland Rock. The lifeboat took two seasick crew board and towed the punt into Padstow.

James Burrough and her crew worked with D class inshore lifeboats from Port Isaac and Rock in a search for survivors after the 137-year-old square-rigged

James Burrough being launched down the slipway at Trevose Head. (By courtesy of the RNLI)

James Burrough pulling the fishing vessel Ross Alcedo, of Panama, to safety on 20 April 1987 after it went aground near Newquay. (By courtesy of Padstow RNLI)

sailing ship *Maria Asumpta* went ashore on the Pentire Point on 30 May 1995. The ship, one of the oldest sailing vessels afloat, was entering the Camel estuary in a fresh north-westerly breeze when she hit rocks on the eastern side of the entrance, near Rumps Point. She began to break up almost immediately. *James Burrough* launched at 4.37pm and Port Isaac ILB was launched to make the three-mile passage to the scene. Both boats were on scene within half an hour, but there was little they could do to stop the vessel becoming a wreck. Of the fourteen people aboard, all but three had already been picked up by fishing vessels or climbed the cliffs of the point by the time the lifeboats arrived. A helicopter soon recovered

James Burrough approaching the slipway prior to being recovered after a publicity launch, August 1989. (Nicholas Leach)

the body of one person from the casualty and both lifeboats searched for two other people who were unnaccounted for, but without success.

On 13 January 1996 *James Burrough* was launched under the command of Coxswain Alan Tarby to assist the fishing vessel *Try Again*, which was taking in water. By the time the lifeboat arrived on scene, the water level had risen so high that the skipper had to shut down his engine, thus meaning his pumps did not work, while heavy seas constantly hit the vessel. One of the lifeboat's crew went aboard the casualty to operate the lifeboat's pump, and two of the fishing vessel's crew were transferred to the lifeboat. The casualty was taken in tow and by 10pm the pump had lowered the water level sufficiently so that the main engine could be restarted and the on-board pump could be used. The tow was released, and the lifeboat then escorted the casualty into Padstow. Although this was a straightforward operation in many respects, the sea state made it hazardous and difficult, and the casualty would have been in serious trouble had the lifeboat not responded so quickly.

Soon after this service the relief lifeboat *Owen and Anne Aisher* arrived for a short stint, staying form February 1996 until 21 May 1996 while *James Burrough* went for a survey at Appledore Shipyard. The relief boat performed one service during her stay at Trevose Head. *James Burrough* returned in late May and had a busy summer, assisting several yachts and motor boats before going to Souters Shipyard at Cowes for another survey with another relief lifeboat, *Voluntary Worker*, taking her place in mid-December. The second relief boat of 1996 stayed until April 1997, completing seven services during that time, four of which were to fishing vessels. On 7 April 1997 *James Burrough* returned from a refit at Souters. Soon after leaving Cowes on her return journey, she was called to two emergencies in the Solent. Once clear of these, she carried on to Weymouth, but

James Burrough exercising with a Sea King helicopter from RNAS Culdrose during a demonstation at Newquay. (Paul Richards)

On board James Burrough are, back row left to right, Dr Mike Rees (lifeboat doctor), Peter Lobb, Chris Hughes, Tim Lloyd and Alan Tarby; front row left to right, Ricky Tummon (Second Coxswain), Eddie Murt (Mechanic), Trevor England (Coxswain), Edward Hicks and Bill Tippett (Assistant Mechanic). (By courtesy of Padstow RNLI)

before reaching harbour she went to a French yacht, which she towed in.

In August 1997 *James Burrough* assisted three yachts, the last of which was the 21ft cutter *Sea Bear*, which went aground at Polzeath on 23 August 1997. The two people on board managed to step ashore, while the Padstow and Rock lifeboats arrived on scene to recover the vessel. A pump was taken aboard the casualty, which was towed to Padstow after being refloated. Polzeath auxiliary coastguards were also involved in the incident, which was showed how well the different services could work together.

On 6 September 1998 the Padstow lifeboat crew were involved in a major rescue operation at Bossiney Cove after the Port Isaac inshore lifeboat got trapped in a cave while trying to rescue two stranded swimmers. The ILB had attempted to save the two stranded people, but was overwhelmed by heavy swell and breaking seas at the mouth of the cave, which resulted in the boat being wrecked and two of the three crew members on board becoming trapped in the cave close to the two casualties. The third crew member was airlifted to safety by a helicopter from RNAS Culdrose. *James Burrough* was also launched to help and her crew spent four hours standing by a short distance off the cliffs in appalling conditions while waiting for the tide to turn so that the four trapped people could escape. At about 9.30pm the tide had had fallen enough for the crew members inside the cave to help the casualties towards the inside of the entrance and for the Coastguard team to reach the outside. All four came out safely with only relatively minor injuries and they were airlifted to hospital.

The lifeboat crew were shocked, badly bruised and suffering from inhaling petrol fumes, but were discharged later that night. The casualties were also shocked and bruised, and were suffering from hypothermia. Coxswain Alan Tarby said afterwards: 'It was a tremendous joint effort and all credit is due to Coastguard Sector Officer Frank Jones and his teams.' Their efforts earned

Donor of James Burrough, Heather 'Mickie' Allen, in the crew room of the Trevose Head boathouse on 17 August 1998 receiving a birthday cake from the crew. Pictured, from left to right, are John Alldridge (Mechanic), Mike England (Assistant Mechanic), Alan Tarby (Coxswain), Brian Hawes, and crew members Chris O'Neill, Peter Rojano and Andrew Parsons. (Nicholas Leach)

them an official Letter of Thanks from the Director of the RNLI, while Port Isaac helmsman Kevin Dingle and crew member Mike Edkins were accorded the Thanks on Vellum. Five Coastguard rescue teams had turned out for the emergency, with two sets of managers and three lifeboats.

Exactly a year after the incident at Bossiney Cove, on 6 September 1999, *James Burrough* was launched to assist the 55ft fishing vessel *Defiant*, which was taking in water at Pentire Point. Despite very poor visibility, the lifeboat reached the casualty, whose crew had run the vessel aground until the arrival of the lifeboat. The lifeboat transferred two crew members with water pumps across to the casualty to pump out water from the fish room and forward section. The casualty was then able to make passage slowly up the estuary towards Padstow, but had difficulty steering due to the amount of water in the forward section. A tow was passed, but as the casualty was sheering considerably the tow had to be released.

James Burrough being launched for lifeboat day, August 1998. (Nicholas Leach)

The rope then fouled under the casualty and had to be slipped. The casualty was slowly escorted by the lifeboat to Padstow, where the fire brigade took over pumping until the water receded. This was the first time that the lifeboat crew had used the RNLI's pump and it saved the fishing vessel from sinking.

On 30 October 1999 *James Burrough* was involved in a challenging rescue, launching at 4.30pm to the 55ft fishing boat *Charisma*, which had broken down thirty miles off Trevose Head. The vessel had problems with her gearbox and needed to be brought in for repairs to be carried out, so the lifeboat launched at 4.30pm and made best speed for the casualty. The lifeboat took *Carisma*, with five crew aboard, in tow and headed back towards Padstow. The passage back proved to be relatively uneventful until the weather and seas began to worsen.

A helicopter winching exercise with James Burrough off the harbour for lifeboat day, August 1998. (Nicholas Leach)

James Burrough in the river Camel off Padstow harbour during a helicopter winching demonstration, with the winchman at the stern awaiting to be lifted back to the helicopter. (Nicholas Leach)

James Burrough exercising with an RAF helicopter at Appledore. (By courtesy of Padstow RNLI)

As the two vessels reached the mouth of the estuary and crossed Doom Bar, a 15ft wave hit the boat, smashing a wheelhouse window and buckling the stanchions. It also caused the towrope to break, injuring two of the Padstow crew, Bernard Murt and Neil Simpson, but not seriously.

The St Ives lifeboat was called to help and took over the tow to keep *Charisma* from going aground while *James Burrough* returned to station where the injured crewmen were landed and fresh crew and another tow rope were picked up. *James Burrough* then returned to the casualty and, assisted by St Ives lifeboat, fixed up another tow line and brought *Charisma* back into Padstow in the early hours of the following morning. The lifeboat returned to station having spent over seventeen hours at sea undertaking a rescue which was made very difficult by the sudden worsening of the weather. One crew member later said that the sea had been flat one minute and then heavy the next, whipped up by a westerly force eight or nine wind. Following this incident, *James Burrough* went to Appledore Shipyard for repairs on 3 November and the relief 47ft Tyne *The Famous Grouse* arrived, staying for less than a fortnight.

Lifeboat day demonstration at Newquay with James Burrough exercising with a Sea King helicopter from RNAS Culdrose while Newquay's Atlantic 75 ILB B-715 Phyllis and C class inflatable stand by.

James Burrough with, left to right, Brian Hawes, Robert Norfolk (head launcher), Bernard Murt, Tim Norfolk, Richard Pitman, John Alldridge (Mechanic), Jason Nicholas, Chris Murphy, Mike England, Dr White (LMA), Alan Tarby (Coxswain), Edward Hicks (Second Coxswain) and George Phillips (LOM). (By courtesy of Padstow RNLI)

In 2001 *James Burrough* and her crew experienced a particularly busy year, with the first launch coming on 14 January when they went to assist the eighty-five-tonne fishing vessel *Admiral Gordon*, which had machinery failure. A month later the lifeboat went to another fishing vessel, *Cornish Maid*, which also had machinery failure, and on 11 March the 18m yacht *Schiemallion* was towed to safety from just outside Newquay harbour after the vessel's steering had failed. On 8 April *James Burrough* was called out again, this time launching to assist the motor cruisers *Intuition* and *Evado*, which were caught out in bad weather. The vessels were found about fifteen miles north-west of Padstow, struggling to cope in the force four to five winds. Once communication had been established by the lifeboat crew with the casualties, and after ascertaining everyone on board was well, they were given a course to steer to Padstow and were escorted safely over the Doom Bar and into harbour. Launching late in the evening on 31 August 2001, *James Burrough* went to the catamaran *Wildwind*, whose sole occupant was in need of medical assistance, twenty-five miles south-west of

James Burrough and St Ives lifeboat bringing in the fishing vessel Charisma on 30 October 1999. (By courtesy of Padstow RNLI)

Pentire. Two lifeboat crewmembers went aboard the catamaran once the lifeboat reached the scene, and first aid was administered, while the man was made as comfortable and stable as possible, while the vessel was towed into Padstow. The vessels reached harbour at 3.25am, to be met by an ambulance and paramedics, with the lifeboat returning to the boathouse at 5am on 1 September.

On 8 August 2002 *James Burrough* went to the aid of the yacht *Bryn Mawr*, which got into difficulties just before midnight on 7 August 2002 after her propeller and rudder were fouled by crab pot ropes. The lifeboat put out just after midnight in moderate seas and force four winds and found the casualty being blown towards cliffs, having dropped anchor in an attempt to stay in a safe position while awaiting help. The lifeboat arrived alongside the vessel at 12.20am and passed a rope across. The weight was taken off her anchor, which the yacht's crew retrieved and the tow commenced. The lifeboat pulled *Bryn Mawr* further out to sea and awaited sufficient water to safely enter the river. Just before half tide, after the crew fired parachute flares to illuminate the area, the lifeboat crossed the bar and took the yacht into Padstow harbour, where she was safely berthed. The lifeboat returned to station at 3.35am on 8 August. After the service, a letters of thanks was received from the rescued, and the owners of *Bryn Mawr* wrote to the crew thanking them for their services, stating that, until then, 'in all my years experience of the sea I have, luckily, never had to be rescued'.

In November 2002 the relief lifeboat *Sarah Emily Harrop* arrived at the station with *James Burrough* going for refit at Seagleam yard at Bembridge, Isle of Wight. The work on her involved her being repainted inside and out, her engines reconditioned and new navigation and communication equipment fitted. The relief boat, which was originally stationed at Lytham St Annes, undertook two services before the end of the year, the second of which, on 19 December 2002, saw her launch to the merchant vessel *Sena Deniz*, which had been disabled by a fire in her engine room. Along with the St Ives lifeboat and a helicopter from RNAS Culdrose, *Sarah Emily Harrop* was launched to help. The casualty had a crew of twenty-four, only one of whom spoke any English. Crew members Steve Conium and Richard Jay went aboard the vessel to give first aid treatment to some of the crew who had been burnt trying to fight the fire, while another man suffering from the effects of smoke was given oxygen. The helicopter went to Falmouth to pick up a fire-fighting team and a doctor, and two of the casualties were flown to hospital for treatment while the firemen supervised the damping down of the fire. The lifeboats were released from the scene once the situation was under control and *Sarah Emily Harrop* returned to station.

James Burrough completed her refit in March 2003 and was launched from the boatyard on 17 March. After successful engine and equipment trials, she was passed out ready to return to Padstow on 4 April. During the summer *James Burrough* assisted a couple of fishing boats and yachts, and on 31 October 2003 was needed for a very quick launch after an angler was washed into the sea. With a heavy ground swell of four to five metres to contend with, the shore crew worked quickly and skilfully to launch *James Burrough* at 8.52am, within eight minutes of the pagers going off. The lifeboat was on scene seven minutes after launching and, in good visibility with force three winds but a rough sea, began searching for the missing angler hard. The lifeboat got to within 200m of the cliff and the crowd, which had assembled at the location, pointed out the man and, as the lifeboat rose on top of a wave, the crew spotted the casualty about 25m away. When the angler fell in the water, he had had the presence of mind and strength to swim away from the cliffs rather than try to swim back in.

James Burrough at the head of the slipway at Trevose Head prior to launching on exercise. (By courtesy of Padstow RNLI)

James Burrough leaving Poole bound for her last refit at Bembridge Isle of Wight. (Peter Edey)

James Burrough out of the water at Seagleam, Bembridge, Isle of Wight, on 14 March 2003, after her last refit. (Peter Edey)

Coxswain Alan Tarby later commented: 'He would almost certainly have been badly hurt or even killed by the force of the sea breaking onto the rocks.'

The angler was exhausted when the lifeboat reached him and so when the crew threw him a heaving line he was too weak to use it. Coxswain Tarby then manoeuvred the lifeboat alongside him and crew members Chris Murphy and Kevin Briggs climbed down the scrambling net to grab the angler and, with the help of other crew, lift him on board the lifeboat. As the casualty was showing signs of hypothermia, he was placed in the recovery position, wrapped in blankets and given oxygen. However, his condition deteriorated quickly, he was vomiting and drifting in and out of consciousness. A helicopter from RNAS Culdrose arrived on scene and agreed to try to airlift the casualty to hospital at Truro. With some difficulty, due to the heavy swell, the helicopter winchman was landed on the lifeboat's deck with a stretcher, with the casualty being given first aid until he was successfully lifted by the helicopter. After the man was taken by the helicopter to hospital, Coxswain Tarby recalls, 'there was a great feeling that we had achieved something worthwhile'. In letters to the lifeboat and shore crews, Operations Director Michael Vlasto commented: 'This was a first-class team effort, demonstrating fast response, excellent first aid and polished team work.' The angler's life had been saved, and he subsequently made a full recovery.

The year 2004 started quietly before the lifeboat was called on several times during a busy August and September. Of the three launches in August, one was to assist during the flooding at Boscastle, an event which made the national news headlines when the village suffered extensive damage after flash floods caused by an exceptional amount of rain that fell over eight hours that afternoon. *James Burrough* spent more than twelve hours away from her station searching for possible missing people. She launched at 4.55am and was on scene by first light, searching in the entrance to Boscastle amongst considerable debris but nothing was found. Once the search was finished, the crew was asked to recover an upturned vessel, which was in danger of breaking up inside the harbour entrance so the vessel was towed to deeper water and pumped out. After landing the vessel, the lifeboat returned to station twelve and a half hours after launching.

During the summer two relief boats came to the station for short stints. The first boat, *Mariner's Friend*, came in July so that *James Burrough's* cooling system could be repainted, which mean the station was non-operational. It was possible to keep the relief boat on a mooring because of favourable tidal conditions, while *James Burrough* remained in the boathouse, where the work was carried out more easily and cheaply than if she had been taken to a boatyard. The second time, when work on the bilge keel was required, something that could only be done in a yard, saw another relief Tyne, *St Cybi II (Civil Service No.40),* coming to the station. The boat was built for Holyhead and, despite being the next boat

James Burrough inside the lifeboat house at the head of the slipway. (By courtesy of Padstow RNLI)

The air-bags on the aft cabin of James Burrough. They were fitted to ensure that, should she be capsized, she would definitely right herself.

to *James Burrough* in the Tyne build programme, the crew noted a number of differences in the two boats.

The first service of 2005 was undertaken on 19 February when *James Burrough* was launched at 4.45pm to assist the 23m fishing vessel *Francis of Ladram*, which had engine failure. In the fresh northerly wind and neap tide, towing the casualty into Padstow would have been difficult so, as the closest safe harbour was Newlyn, *James Burrough* towed the vessel towards Land's End where Sennen Cove lifeboat took over and completed the tow to Newlyn. The two lifeboats rendezvoused seven miles north of Pendeen, where the tow was transferred. Padstow lifeboat then returned to station after seven and a half hours at sea.

Towards the end of the year *James Burrough* was involved in assisting two other fishing vessels, *Intuition* and *Diligence*. On 20 October 2005 she launched at 1.34pm to the 20m *Intuition* which had gearbox failure twelve miles north of Padstow with seven persons onboard. The lifeboat arrived on scene within an

The lifeboat house and slipway at Trevose Head were built in 1965-67 and used throughout James Burrough's service career at Padstow. Major repairs were carried out to the substructures of both the boathouse and slipway in 1991. (Nicholas Leach)

Edward Hicks, Peter Lobb, Mike England and Alan Tarby on board James Burrough in July 2006 at the RNLI Depot, Poole

hour of launching and towed her safely into Padstow harbour. Two days later *James Burrough* went to help the same 20m fishing boat which had again suffered gearbox failure, so the lifeboat towed her in again. As *James Burrough* was being washed down inside the boathouse following this incident, she was called out again, to another fishing vessel, this time one owned by lifeboat crew member Brian Bate. The boat had a fouled propeller and so the lifeboat put out at 1.38pm and was alongside the casualty just after 2pm. Two lifeboat crew managed to remove the ropes and the casualty reached harbour without further assistance.

The last few services performed by *James Burrough* all proved to be routine in nature, with the four in June 2006 all to help pleasure craft of various

James Burrough at sea off Stepper Point to meet her successor, Spirit of Padstow, in July 2006. A few days after this, she left the station for the last time and was sold for service in China. (Nicholas Leach)

descriptions. Her final service was undertaken on 12 July when she launched at 8.30pm to the 10m yacht *Avianta*, which was on her way from Alicante to South Wales and had fouled her propeller. The wind was too light for her to make her way into Padstow unaided at low water and so she requested a tow. The lifeboat was alongside within thirty minutes and safely took her up the estuary to the lifeboat mooring in the pool. They then arranged for the harbour staff to take her up to the quay on the next high tide.

Following this service, *James Burrough* remained on station for only a few more days before her successor took over duties. She left Padstow for the last time on 29 July 2006 manned by Coxswain Alan Tarby, Mechanic Michael England, Second Coxswain Edward Hicks and Emergency Mechanic Peter Lobb. The four crew members' service totalled over 100 years between them, and Second Coxswain Hicks retired from the crew with the departure of the Tyne after twenty-nine years of service. The crew took *James Burrough* to Poole, and said farewell to her on 30 July. After a few months in the Relief Fleet, she was sold out of service to the China Salvage & Rescue Bureau and was shipped to China on board a container ship out of Felixstowe, which left the English port on 8 August 2007. Once she reached China, she was renamed *Huaying 387* and was operated as a lifeboat at Rongcheng Base.

Spirit of Padstow

Wwhile *James Burrough* was in the final few years of her operational service at Padstow, plans were being made to modernise the station with the provision of not only a new lifeboat but also a new lifeboat house. In January 2004 it was announced that the station was to receive a new Tamar class lifeboat, while the RNLI trustees gave the go ahead for a £5.5 million contract to build a new boathouse at Trevose Head, overlooking Mother Ivey's Bay, to house the new boat. Maritime engineering specialists John Martin Construction of Norfolk, who had completed a new wave break to protect the lifeboat berth at Walton and Frinton, undertook the construction work on the new house and slipway, which were designed by architects Poynton Bradbury Wynter Cole of St Ives with Haskoning UK Ltd as consulting engineers. The new building was the second lifeboat house and slipway to be built specifically for the new Tamar design after one at Tenby had been completed in 2005.

The complex construction project involved overcoming considerable difficulties due to the very restricted access, exposed location and the Cornish holiday traffic. Construction was carried out using a large jack-up barge, with ninety per cent of the building materials being brought by sea as the roads leading to the station were unsuitable for HGV transportation. An exception was made for the delivery of over 700 tonnes of premix concrete for the

Spirit of Padstow under construction at DML, Plymoth. (By courtesy of Padstow RNLI)

main deck slab. Several pours were necessary during summer 2005 and work was scheduled during the night to enable the trucks to arrive unhindered and without disrupting traffic to local caravan parks. The largest concrete pump in the country was deployed to pump the concrete from the cliff top to site several hundred feet below.

The main building, of a simple C-shaped design, was of a timber frame construction built on large laminated timber ribs, and the curved copper roof was made to weather to a green colour to blend in with the surroundings. The new slipway is 75m in length with a gradient of one in five, enabling the lifeboat to launch into a minimum depth of 2.6m of water. Construction of the distinctively shaped boathouse and slipway took only fourteen months and it was built alongside the existing boathouse, the modernisation of which was deemed to be too difficult and costly. *James Burrough* remained operational throughout the construction period operating from the old house. The new

The 1967 lifeboat house and slipway at Trevose Head with the piling for the new station in place alongside, June 2005. (Nicholas Leach)

The jack-up barge in place while work takes place on the new lifeboat house adjacent to the 1967 lifeboat house and slipway. The barge was used for forty of the seventy-four weeks of the project. (By courtesy of Padstow RNLI)

The new lifeboat house starts to take shape, with the curved copper roof on a wooden framework visible behind the boathouse it was replacing. (By courtesy of Padstow RNLI)

The new boathouse dwarfs the old house as it nears completion. It is almost twice the size of the old one and incorporates a tipping cradle, so that the boat can be kept level for ease of maintenance, training rooms, showers and toilets and improved changing rooms. (By courtesy of Padstow RNLI)

house was completed in summer 2006, several months ahead of schedule, and was opened to the public for the first time in August. It subsequently won two prestigious awards, being named winner of the new building category at the Cornish Building Group Awards in February 2007 and three months later it won the Local Authority Building Control Award in the best public/community project category for the south west of England.

While the new house was under construction, the new Tamar lifeboat was being fitted out at Plymouth. The Tamar design was the culmination of several years of work by design teams from the RNLI engineering office and Devonport Management Ltd in Plymouth. The hull was of composite construction, made from glass and epoxy resin with a foam core sandwich structure above the water.

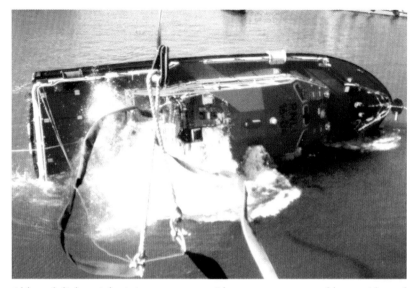

Capsze trials of Spirit of Padstow at DML, Plymouth. (By courtesy of Padstow RNLI)

Although lightweight, it is very strong, with one square metre able to withstand a force of sixty-eight tonnes. The boat was built in two halves, which were stuck together; the deck and wheelhouse were a single moulding, made upside down and then turned over and stuck on top of the hull. The boat is driven by two Caterpillar C18 marine diesel engines, each of 1,015hp, powering two propellers to give a top speed of twenty-five knots, and providing her with a considerable towing capability. The top speed can be maintained for up to ten hours, giving the boat a range of 125 miles, and to achieve this she carries 1,000 gallons of fuel. The Tamar carries a small inflatable Y class boat, which is used for rescues in shallow areas, close to rocks or caves and to transfer personnel, and is stowed under the deck at the stern of the boat. The five seats in the wheelhouse are fitted with flat screens, which form the interface for the integrated electronic

Padstow crew on the new 16m Tamar Spirit of Padstow at Poole during the crew training. On board are, left to right, Guy Richards (Poole Training Deptartment), Andrew Woods (RNLI), Alan Tarby, Ian Kitto, Michael England, Steve Nicholas, Oliver Vivian and Robert Lee (Poole trainer). (By courtesy of Padstow RNLI)

The new and old boathouses at Trevose Head with the old one still in operational use. (By courtesy of Padstow RNLI)

Systems and Information Management System (SIMS) that gives easy access to information about the boat's systems.

The new lifeboat, the fourth of the class, was funded, like her predecessor, by Miss Heather B. Allen and was named *Spirit of Padstow*. She arrived at Padstow on 3 July 2006 with the frigate HMS *Cornwall*, which was circumnavigating Cornwall, on hand to greet the craft. After reaching Padstow bar at 12 noon, she was escorted into the small harbour by her predecessor, 47ft Tyne *James Burrough* and D class inflatable D-634 *Rusper* from Rock on the opposite side of the Camel Estuary, and a flotilla of small craft. After overnight stops at Fowey and the Isles of Scilly, she arrived at Padstow where crowds of well-wishers thronged the small harbour and applauded as the new lifeboat passed the end of the pier and moored up near the Harbour Office. During the passage to station from Poole she was manned by Coxswain Alan Tarby, Mechanic Michael England, and crew members Steve Nicholas, Ian Kitto and Oliver Vivian. Inspector Simon Pryce and Divisional Engineer Andrew Woods were also on board during the trip.

Later in the day, *Spirit of Padstow* was taken to Trevose Head for slipway launching trails and tests at the new boathouse. On her arrival at the new slipway, she was hauled out of the water stern first, some adjustments were made to the tipping cradle with her sitting on it, and she was then launched for the first time. After a second trial launch, she was kept on a mooring overnight and was not kept permanently in the new boathouse until it was completed and had been handed over, which took place towards the end of July. During July, a series of crew training passages were undertaken to train the volunteer crew members in operating their new craft before she officially took over from the Tyne. Once the intensive crew training had been completed, *Spirit of Padstow* was placed on service at Padstow on 17 July 2006.

The new lifeboat was officially named and dedicated at a ceremony in Padstow harbour on Sunday 17 September 2006. The Mayor of Padstow, Cllr Keith Freeman, welcomed guests and John Stephens, Chairman of the station, opened the proceedings. The new lifeboat house was officially opened by Admiral Sir Jock Slater, Chairman of the RNLI, after which Peter Shone, a friend of the late Miss Mickie Allen, formally handed over the lifeboat to the RNLI. The boat was accepted by Andrew Freemantle, RNLI Chief Executive, and passed into the care of the station's Lifeboat Operations Manager, Michael Walker. The service of dedication was conducted by the Rt Rev Roydon Screech, Bishop of St Germans, assisted by Padstow Lifeboat Chaplains. At the

During her call at Fowey in July 2006, Spirit of Padstow joined a number of former lifeboats which were involved in an annual get together of such craft. She was moored at the lifeboat pontoon with Fowey lifeboat Maurice and Joyce Hardy and former lifeboat William Cantrell Ashley. (Nicholas Leach)

Spirit of Padstow
entering the Camel
Estuary for the first
time, 3 July 2006.
(Nicholas Leach)

Spirit of Padstow
arriving on station,
3 July 2006,
escorted by James
Burrough and Rock
inshore lifeboat
D-634 Rusper.
(Nicholas Leach)

Spirit of Padstow
is led towards
Padstow harbour
by James Burrough,
3 July 2006.
(Nicholas Leach)

The new 16m Tamar Spirit of Padstow arriving on station on 3 July 2006 is met by James Burrough off Stepper Point before being escorted into harbour. (Nicholas Leach)

James Burrough arriving at Padstow for the first time, 3 July 2006, passing HMS Cornwall at the mouth of the Camel Estuary. (Nicholas Leach)

The new and old
lifeboat houses
at Trevose Head.
(Nicholas Leach)

Spirit of Padstow
being recovered
up the slipway
for the first time,
3 July 2006.
(Nicholas Leach)

Spirit of Padstow
being hauled up
the new slipway for
the first time; the
fitting out of the
new boathouse was
in its final stages.
(Nicholas Leach)

Spirit of Padstow with James Burrough in the harbour as crowds of well-wishers watched the new lifeboat arrive at her station, 3 July 2006. (Nicholas Leach)

end of the ceremony the boat was formally christened by Mr Shone and she then put out for a short trip in the estuary.

Spirit of Padstow's first service call came before she had become operational at Padstow. On 14 July 2006 several crew members were coming to the end of four days of familiarisation training aboard the new boat and were just outside Milford Haven when a call was received that a 19ft Cornish shrimper yacht had become entangled with plastic sheeting debris. The debris had fouled her propeller and this, together with the heavy weather, meant that her four crew were unable to make way under sail. Deputy Second Coxswain James Chown immediately headed for the stricken yacht and, once alongside, he put crew members Steve Conium and Tom Norfolk aboard the yacht to prepare a towline. The casualty was secured and then towed into Milford Haven, where it was safely berthed.

Once on station and officially the Padstow lifeboat, *Spirit of Padstow* performed her first effective service on 5 August 2006. She was being prepared to go on her first public relations trip to Newquay for their lifeboat day when she was called to assist the Newquay Atlantic 75 ILB which was towing in a broken down motor cruiser. The 12.6m traditionally-built boat, with three persons onboard, had suffered engine failure two miles west of the Madrips in Holywell Bay. Due to the size of the vessel, Falmouth coastguard was unsure if the Atlantic would be able to tow the casualty for any distance so assistance from the Tamar was requested. Spirit of Padstow was launched on what was her first service call

Spirit of Padstow is hauled up the slipway of the new lifeboat house at Trevose Head, 3 July 2006. (Nicholas Leach)

The first launch of Spirit of Padstow from the new lifeboat house at Trevose Head. (Nicholas Leach)

from Padstow and met the casualty with Newquay lifeboat already on scene. She took over the tow and brought the vessel to the lifeboat mooring in the Pool before being rehoused late in the evening. At 10am the following morning Spirit of Padstow was launched again and returned to Newquay to take part in the lifeboat day demonstrations as planned

On 13 August 2006 the new boathouse was open to the public for the first time and a record number of people visited it and looked over the new Spirit of Padstow. The lifeboat launched at 3.30pm to cheers from the watching crowd and applause when she was recovered. But after a very busy day at the station, when everyone had gone home, the crew's pagers went off and Falmouth Coastguard requested the lifeboat be launched after St Merryn Coastguard had been alerted to a possible dead body seen floating in the sea at Warren Cove, just south of Treyarnon Bay. By 8.20pm the lifeboat was afloat and heading

Spirit of Padstow
arriving at the
harbour for her
naming ceremony,
17 September 2006.
(Paul Richards)

The champagne bottle breaks over the bow of Spirit of Padstow at the end of her naming ceremony, 17 September 2006. (Paul Richards)

Lifeboat crew on board Spirit of Padstow for her naming ceremony, 17 September 2006 are, left to right, Richard Pitman, Brian Bate, Neil Simpson, Stevie Conium, James Chown, Coxswain Alan Tarby, Chris Murphy and Mechanic Michael England. (Paul Richards)

for the area. She arrived on scene soon afterwards and the crew were directed towards the cove by Coastguards already on scene. Coxswain Tarby decided to use the Y boat to help with the search, so crew members Richard Pitman and Ross McBurnie donned dry suits and launched the Y boat from the stern of the Tamar. Having located the object in the water, they realised that it was not a body but a large amount of netting which they pulled onboard the Y boat. This was then recovered onto the lifeboat and the boat was able to return to station.

During her first full year on station, *Spirit of Padstow* was involved in a particularly fine rescue. At 11.08am on 25 June 2007 Falmouth Coastguard requested the launch of the lifeboat to go to the aid of the yacht *Coresande*, which was in difficulties four miles north of Trevose Head in north-westerly force eight to nine winds. The 40ft yacht, with two people on board, had a blown out sail, was taking on water and was unable to sail. The lifeboat and slipway were made

ready for an immediate launch and at 11.20am *Spirit of Padstow* hit the water, crewed by Coxswain Alan Tarby, Mechanic Michael England, Second Mechanic Chris Murphy, and crew members Neil Simpson, Steve Nicholas, Luke Chown, Ian Kitto, David Flide and Tom Norfolk. On rounding Trevose Head, the lifeboat met the full force of the weather. Best speed was made towards the casualty, which was in danger of sinking, with the lifeboat averaging fifteen knots over the ground as she travelled the four miles to the yacht. The waves were estimated to be three to four metres high, many of them breaking, with a heavy 10m ground swell running from the west.

At 11.42am the lifeboat arrived at the casualty which was lying towards the

Spirit of Padstow off Trevose Head on the afternoon of 25 June 2007, after the service to the yacht Corusande; the lifeboat could not get back on the slipway due to the bad weather. (By courtesy of the RNLI)

16m Tamar Spirit of Padstow on exercise off the North Cornish coast. (RNLI/Nigel Millard)

west. No sails were set and she was rolling heavily, while both crew were in the cockpit. Water had risen to just above the cabin sole and the pump had stopped working. Coxswain Tarby decided that two crewmen should go aboard the yacht and her crew taken off prior to attempting to save the boat, and crew members Luke Chown and Chris Murphy volunteered to transfer to the yacht. Coxswain Tarby manoeuvred the lifeboat alongside the casualty and crewman Murphy was transferred. The lifeboat then backed away before the manoeuvre was repeated and on the second attempt crewman Chown jumped aboard. Although a towrope was secured from the lifeboat, it proved too dangerous to transfer the yacht's crew to the lifeboat despite the lifeboat being taken alongside the casualty approximately fifteen times. During this time, crew member Chown realised he had injured a finger and was in considerable pain, so Coxswain Tarby requested helicopter assistance and began towing the yacht away from the shore.

The helicopter arrived on scene at 12.45pm and managed to take off the yacht's crew and the two lifeboat crew, despite the heavy swell and the snagging of one of the lines in the yacht's steering gear. Once the yacht was empty,

The small Y class inflatable, crewed by Steve Swabey and Steve Nicholas, being recovered into the stern of Spirit of Padstow. (By courtesy of Padstow RNLI)

the lifeboat altered course and towed it into Padstow, crossing Doom Bar at 2.20pm. Having berthed the yacht, and while returning to the boathouse to assess recovery conditions, the lifeboat was tasked to another yacht, which was aground at Trebetherick Point on the eastern side of the estuary. The vessel, the 30ft sloop Fly, had fouled her anchor and was in a treacherous position, made worse by the falling tide, gale force winds and rough seas. Arriving at the back of the bar, the lifeboat crew saw the yacht was well aground on the rocks clear of the water, but in the prevailing conditions the lifeboat could not get close, so she stood by outside the bar.

The yachtsman was persuaded to abandon his vessel, but during the lifeboat's approach, the motion of the yacht caused it to hit the lifeboat. The force of the impact caused the yachtsman to fall overboard and, though he remained secured by his safety harness, it took several minutes to recover him. It was too rough for the lifeboat to cross Doom Bar and get to harbour with the casualty, so having taken the sole occupant off, the lifeboat headed for open after and awaited helicopter evacuation of the survivor, which was completed about half an hour later after the helicopter had completed a service off St Ives. As conditions were too bad at Trevose to attempt to recover the lifeboat, at 10.30pm she was taken across the bar and into the harbour to be refuelled and put on the pool mooring. The crew came ashore at 11.35pm and the lifeboat was recovered onto the slipway the next day, when conditions improved.

Following these two dramatic rescues, Coxswain Alan Tarby was accorded the Thanks of the Institution on Vellum, while crew members Luke Chown and Christopher Murphy received framed letters of thanks from the Chairman of the RNLI for their part in the incidents. Tom Mansell, RNLI Deputy Divisional Inspector, says Alan Tarby and his volunteer crew ensured the eleven hours spent at sea were used to best effect in rescuing all three people: 'This was a long, dangerous and difficult service in which Coxswain Alan Tarby displayed

Spirit of Padstow breaks through the surf off Bude beach off Bude RNLI's annual lifeboat day in 2008. Padstow lifeboat crew regularly attend lifeboat days in support of neighbouring stations. (By courtesy of Padstow RNLI)

first class seamanship, decision making, determination and courage. He was well supported by the excellent teamwork of his volunteer crew, two of whom, Chris Murphy and Luke Chown, transferred to the first yacht. These two showed considerable courage in undertaking this task willingly in such dangerous conditions.' Mechanic Michael England and volunteer crew members, Neil Simpson, Steven Nicholas, Ian Kitto, David Flide and Thomas Norfolk each received an individual letter of appreciation signed by RNLI Chief Executive Andrew Freemantle.

After the drama of the double rescue in June 2007, the services undertaken during the rest of the year were relatively routine in nature, with a number of broken down fishing vessels assisted while towards the end of the year the Relief Tamar *Frank and Anne Wilkinson* was on station, from 3 to 18 November 2007. In 2008 the summer proved to be the busiest period for the station, with a number of rescues completed. On 1 July *Spirit of Padstow* went to the 15m yacht Salamander, with three persons on board, after the vessel suffered gearbox failure. On 22 July the lifeboat was called to help the fishing vessel *Viking*, which had two persons onboard and which had also suffered gearbox failure. She was fifteen miles south-west of Trevose Head and was towed back to Padstow. On 30 July , during the annual lifeboat day, *Spirit of Padstow* was called away to assist the occupants of the French yacht *Sparky*, which was twelve miles south west of Trevose Head. The yacht had left Cork and had experienced heavy weather the previous night leaving the four French occupants cold, wet and extremely fatigued. On arriving on scene two lifeboat crew were transferred to the yacht and all four of the yacht's crew were taken on board the lifeboat where they were

The relief Tamar
Edward and Barbara
Prigmore moored
in the harbour. She
served at Padstow
for two stints in
2009. (By courtesy of
Padstow RNLI)

The relief Tamar
Edward and
Barbara Prigmore
at moorings off
Trevose Head. (By
courtesy of Padstow
RNLI)

The relief Tamar
Edward and Barbara
Prigmore arriving
at the station.
(By courtesy of
Padstow RNLI)

Padstow lifeboat crew in 2010; back row, left to right, Ross McBurnie, Alan Hoskin, Luke Chown, Oliver Vivian; middle row: Neil Simpson, Steve Nicholas, Ian Kitto, James Chown, Tom Norfolk, Richard Pitman; front row: Richard Jay, Mike Smith, Alan Tarby (Coxswain), Mike England (Mechanic). (By courtesy of Padstow RNLI)

given dry clothes, blankets and hot drinks. They stayed on the lifeboat as the yacht was towed back to Padstow.

At 11.22am on 26 January 2009 *Spirit of Padstow* was launched in quick time to go to the aid of a kite surfer. A local man had got into difficulties while kite-surfing off Harlyn Bay and in rough seas and strong winds he had been carried out to sea. Despite ditching his board, he was then unable to swim back to shore. The lifeboat was launched and within minutes picked the man out of the water. Medical assistance was given by the volunteer crew and a helicopter then airlifted the man off the lifeboat and transferred him to Treliske for a check up as he had swallowed a large amount of sea water.

Two months later the relief Tamar *Edward and Barbara Prigmore* arrived for a stint of duty which lasted from 7 March to 25 July 2009. She undertook a couple of services while on station, the first on 12 April 2009 to a canoeist and search for a hot air balloon. She launched at 5.04pm after a canoeist had been heard shouting for help in the tide off Dinas Head. The lifeboat found him drifting towards the Quies and immediately took him on board. He was taken towards Constantine where he was landed and the crew watched him until he was in the care of the duty RNLI Lifeguards, who saw him safely ashore. The lifeboat returned to station at 5.39pm, bit was called out again at 9.14pm after several reports had been received of a ditched hot air balloon off Widemouth Bay near Bude.

The lifeboat arrived on scene and searched the area with the assistance of the Bude Coastguard teams ashore but nothing was found and the lifeboat was stood down to return to station at 11.10pm. Later in the year another relief Tamar, *Frank and Anne Wilkinson*, was on station. She stayed from 18 October 2009 to 6 November 2009 while *Spirit of Padstow* was taken to Babcocks at Plymouth for exhaust repairs.

On 14 June 2010 *Spirit of Padstow* launched shortly after 4am to go to the aid of a 26ft sailing yacht with two crew onboard who were experiencing difficulties four miles north of Trevose Head. The sea state was rough with a northerly wind blowing force four to five. Both crew members were suffering from fatigue, seasickness and the onset of hypothermia. On arrival at the vessel, two lifeboat crew were transferred to the yacht to assist, and the lifeboat then

Spirit of Padstow on exercise. (RNLI/ Nigel Millard)

escorted the vessel into Padstow where the yacht's two crew members were met by an ambulance crew for medical treatment. The lifeboat returned to the lifeboat station at 7.30am.

On 4 February 2011 *Spirit of Padstow* was launched to assist in a search for a person thought to have jumped from cliffs at Pentire Point East. Newquay's Atlantic 85 inshore lifeboat, a helicopter and numerous search teams were also involved with the Coastguards on scene concerned for the safety of the Newquay lifeboat because of the large breaking seas. The Tamar rendezvoused with the Newquay lifeboat and worked alongside them. Because of the nature of the call and the sea conditions, the Atlantic remained to the north-east of Towan Head where conditions were more favourable and where local knowledge suggested that the body may drift to. The Padstow boat proceeded to go as close to Pentire Point as was safe and carry out a search there. Because of the seas breaking on the high ground to the west of Pentire, the Tamar could not get very close so a search pattern was undertaken along the tidal drift with Newquay lifeboat inside, but nothing was found and both boats were released to return to station.

On 20 February 2011 *Spirit of Padstow* was launched to assist another neighbouring lifeboat, this time going to help the Port Isaac ILB, which had recovered the crew of the pilot gig *Corsair*. The gig had capsized while trying to enter the harbour in heavy seas. Five people were transferred onto the Tamar while two others, wearing drysuits, remained on board the Port Isaac ILB.

Padstow lifeboat crew on the slipway of the new lifeboat station in 2006, from left to right: Steve Hughes (DLA), Tom Norfolk, Steve Nicholas, Richard Pitman (Second Coxswain), James Chown (Deputy Second Coxswain), Mike England (Mechanic), Neil Simpson, Alan Tarby (Coxswain), Oliver Vivian, Michael Smith (Second Mechanic), Tim Norfolk, Robert Norfolk (Head Launcher), Peter Lobb, Luke Chown and David Flide. (RNLI/Nigel Millard)

The impressive new lifeboat house and slipway off Trevose Head completed in 2006. (RNLI/Nigel Millard)

The impressive lifeboat house at Trevose Head. (Nicholas Leach)

One person had a slight head injury, having been struck by the boat, and all had swallowed sea water. The survivors were all taken below by the Padstow crew, and their wet clothes were removed and replaced by dry ones, and their condition was monitored by crew members on the way back to station. Rescue helicopter 193 then arrived on scene and all the rescued were airlifted off and taken to hospital, allowing the lifeboat to return to station.

On 29 April 2013 the historic former 50ft fishing boat *Courageous II* was making her way to Cornwall to take part in Padstow's Obby Oss Mayday festival celebrations, at which she had been a regular attendee for the previous twenty-five years. However, she ran into trouble just outside Padstow at about 4.45am, running aground on rocks which resulted in her rapid destruction. *Spirit of Padstow* was launched, under Coxswain Alan Tarby, within fifteen minutes and the four crew of *Courageous II* were rescued without a minute to spare, as the boat broke up under their feet. The lifeboat had to be taken in among the rocks to effect the rescue, and Mechanic Mike England said: 'This was a very speedy rescue as the four men were in immediate danger. Fortunately, thanks to skilful boat handling in very shallow water, we were able to get them off the boat and ashore in minutes and they are all well. They're regular visitors to Padstow, and it's very sad to see their boat in such a terrible situation.' The vessel was carrying 900 litres of fuel and coastguards worked with the harbour authority to contain a small oil slick coming from the wreck, while wreckage from the boat was washed up on a local beach. The lifeboat returned to station before 6am with nothing more than a dented propeller.

On 5 May 2013 *Spirit of Padstow* and her crew were involved in a difficult incident, launching at 4.10pm after the six people on the speedboat *Milly* lost control of the boat when she was in the Camel Estuary, near Tregirls beach, and were thrown overboard. Under the command of Coxswain Richard Pitman, with Mechanic Michael England, Navigator Steve Conium and crew Thomas Norfolk, Ross McBurnie, Joseph Small, Kate Simpson and James Swabey, the lifeboat headed to the scene at full speed to help. Rock ILB was already on scene, and the out of control boat was circling at about fifteen knots with nobody on board. From 200m away, local trip boat *Thunder* and some kayakers alerted the Rock ILB crew to the location of the casualties, and the crew made their way towards the casualties to assist.

One of the kayakers, a man in a single kayak, was towing the body of a man who had been hit by *Miffy* after being thrown off the boat. A female kayaker, who was also an off-duty RNLI Casualty Care Trainer, was looking after other casualties, some of whom had been seriously injured. The female kayaker was accompanied in her double kayak by her partner, who was also assisting. Two of the casualties were transferred onto *Thunder*, where an off-duty doctor took over casualty care. The other two were transferred onto Rock ILB. Both vessels returned to Padstow harbour, where the Rock crew provided oxygen to the seriously injured casualties. The emergency services arrived at Padstow harbour and, hearing them approach, Rock Helmsman Mably went to assist the male kayaker who had landed a body on Brea beach.

A local commercial boat skipper and his colleague managed to bring *Milly* under control and towed her to safety. Of the six people on board the speedboat, two lost their lives and two were badly injured. The Padstow crew searched the area for any other casualties before being tasked to the harbour, where the body of the last family member had been found. Two crew members entered the water to recover her body. Once all the casualties had been evacuated from the

16m Tamar Spirit of Padstow on her cradle inside the lifeboat house. (Nicholas Leach)

Spirit of Padstow on exercise with relief D class inflatable D-655 Guardian Angel from Rock, the neighbouring station across the Camel Estuary off Trevose Head, April 2011. (Nicholas Leach)

area, both lifeboats returned to the scene with a change of crew to offer further assistance in recovering items from the water.

A letter of thanks was sent to the crew from RNLI Chairman Charles Hunter-Pease, who write: 'This was a distressing and traumatic service for all involved. The crew demonstrated excellent teamwork, courage and sensitivity throughout. The collective efforts of all involved saved the lives of four people. The crew are to be commended for all that they did. On behalf of the Council of the RNLI, I would like to thank you for your actions. Well done.'

On 7 June 2013 *Spirit of Padstow* was launched at 10.12am, under the command of Deputy Coxswain Mike England, after the 29ft ocean-going rowing boat

George Rawlinson presents the RNLI's Thanks Inscribed on Vellum to Second Coxswain Richard Pitman for the Le Sillon service.

The crew holding certificates were those involved in the service to the French trawler Le Sillon. Left to right: Richard Pitman, Mike England, Oliver Vivian, Luke Chown, Steve Swabey, James Swabey, Mike Dennick, Martin Biddle (LOM) and Alan Hoskin. Standing behind are, left to right, Tom Norfolk, Robert Norfolk, Kevin Briggs, Alan Tarby, and Mike Smith. (By courtesy of Padstow RNLI)

Boudicca, on a race round the British Isles with six persons on board, got into difficulty forty miles north-west of Trevose Head. After a long passage to the casualty, the lifeboat arrived on scene and the rowing boat's crew, who were totally exhausted having been at sea for several days, were taken on board. The craft was then towed back to Padstow. It was a long tow, and Padstow harbour was not reached until almost 6pm.

On 1 February 2014 Padstow lifeboat and her crew performed a fine service after the French trawler *Le Sillon* and her six crew were caught in severe weather and heavy seas. The trawler's wheelhouse windows were smashed and all electronics and machinery failed in atrocious weather, leaving the vessel drifting.

Actor Caroline Quentin visited the station in 2011 while filming an episode or her series 'Caroline Quentin's Cornwall', and boarded Spirit of Padstow. (By courtesy of Padstow RNLI)

A Y class inflatable is kept in the stern of Spirit of Padstow, beneath the deck, being launched down a stern ramp, which is lowered. (Nicholas Leach)

The Y class inflatable Y-201 after being launched from her mother craft, Spirit of Padstow, is used for work inshore. (Nicholas Leach)

Spirit of Padstow launched at 4.08pm under the command of Second Coxswain Richard Pitman, and faced very rough conditions, with seas up to 30ft in height and westerly force eight to nine winds. Once the lifeboat and her crew arrived on scene, they managed to get the vessel under tow as she was drifting towards Trevose Head. Due to the conditions the tow parted as the casualty was being brought clear of Trevose, with the intention to continue towing her north towards Milford Haven. It was impossible to reattach the tow and the six crew wanted to be evacuated from the vessel.

A rescue helicopter was tasked, but it was too rough to get the crew off by lifeboat or to winch them from the deck, so it was decided to get them to jump into the water one by one, from where they could be rescued by the helicopter's winchman. The lifeboat took up a position close by and using its searchlights illuminated the scene. The first five crew were successfully lifted by the helicopter, but they missed the skipper, who was last to jump. He was eventually spotted in the water and recovered by the lifeboat crew. The lifeboat then made its way back to station and was recovered up the slipway in a lull in the heavy seas at 10.17pm. For this rescue, the RNLI's Thanks Inscribed on Vellum was accorded to Second Coxswain Pitman and letters of thanks were sent to the rest of the crew and the shore helpers who recovered the lifeboat. The crew were Mike England (Mechanic), Alan Hoskin, Luke Chown, Oliver Vivian, Steve Swabey and James Swabey.

A service carried out in very challenging conditions took place on 31 May 2015. *Spirit of Padstow* was launched at 5.13pm following reports that a man had been washed into the sea at Trebarwith strand. Deputy Second Coxswain Mike England was in command, and the lifeboat crew face north-westerly force eight to nine winds with very rough seas. The lifeboat arrived on scene and conducted an extensive search of the area, with a rescue helicopter also assisting along with Coastguard teams ashore. However, despite a thorough search nothing was found and the lifeboat returned to station. Due to the state of the sea and the conditions on the slipway the lifeboat and her crew had to wait for a lull in the

Harlyn Bay beach rescue Arancia A-27 being launched by the RNLI's lifeguards for a routine beach patrol, July 2011. (Nicholas Leach)

Lifeguards taking the beach rescue boat A-27 on a routine patrol in Harlyn Bay. This is one of nine beaches in north Cornwall patrolled by RNLI Lifeguards. They form another part of the sea rescue service. (Nicholas Leach)

conditions before it was possible to safely recover. The shore crew on the slipway did an amazing job recovering the boat.

In January 2016 the Padstow lifeboat was involved in a very challenging rescue when the 91m motor vessel *Verity*, carrying 3,000 tonnes of scrap metal to northern Spain, began drifting eight miles offshore in rough seas and force eight winds having lost power a couple of days earlier. At around 11.10pm on 29 January Appledore lifeboat *Mollie Hunt* launched into reasonably choppy seas and headed out to moor off Clovelly. Once there, the crew, who had been monitoring the situation and decided to put to sea in case low tides prevented them getting over Bideford bar, set up two watches so that they could get some rest, and the boat remained there all night.

Spirit of Padstow launched early on 30 January and met *Mollie Hunt* and her crew on scene. The Coastguard had called on a tug to tow *Verity*, but it was coming from Holyhead so was about twenty hours away. As the coaster was drifting and could have ended up ashore, Padstow lifeboat crew set up a tow at 9am and, with support from Appledore, began to pull the vessel round. The tow rope parted once and had to be re-established, but was maintained until 2pm, at which point the Dutch frigate HNLMS *De Ruyter* arrived on scene, having been asked to attend by the Coastguard. The Dutch warship established its own tow and, escorted by both lifeboats, slowly headed towards the shelter of Lundy with *Verity* to await the tug. Appledore lifeboat returned to Clovelly for a complete crew change, assisted by the Clovelly inshore lifeboat, and then returned to the scene and continued to escort the warship and her tow into sheltered waters to the east of Lundy. Padstow crew were then stood down and returned to the

Spirit of Padstow is recovered up the slipway after exercise, April 2011. (Nicholas Leach)

Relief 16m Tamar *Peter and Lesley-Jane Nicholson* towing in the motor yacht *Kingfisher*, 6 August 2013. (RNLI)

station at 9.30pm. The seagoing tug *Bremin Fighter* arrived at approximately 4am on 31 January and set off with *Verity* in tow, heading for Swansea where repairs to the ship could be effected.

The volunteer crews from Padstow and Appledore had spent more than twenty-four hours at sea, battling high winds and big swells to keep the cargo ship and her seven crew safe. Coxswain Alan Tarby said afterwards: 'It was excellent teamwork from the lifeboats, and the skipper and crew from the Dutch Warship did an amazing job in difficult conditions.' Mike Weston, Appledore deputy launching authority, said: 'We needed to make sure the cargo ship didn't drift into shore. She was a bit too close enough for comfort. It was a marathon job for both lifeboat crews, who spent many hours in rough seas keeping the cargo ship safe. A very big swell and gale force winds provided tough conditions and the crews showed a lot skill, grit and determination.'

The lifeboat house and slipway at Trevose Head. (RNLI)

Spirit of Padstow was launched at 9.55pm on 30 March 2018 to assist a yacht five miles north of Trevose Head with three persons on board, one of whom was injured. Coastguard rescue helicopter 924 was also tasked to help locate the yacht as its exact position was unknown, and found the yacht, illuminating the area to assist the lifeboat. Padstow lifeboat arrived on scene at 10.10pm, and two of the lifeboat crew went aboard the yacht to assess the casualty, with the injured person being taken on board the lifeboat. Another of the yacht's crew was transferred to the lifeboat, leaving two lifeboat crew and the third of the casualty's crew on the yacht. A tow was rigged and the yacht was brought to Padstow, with lifeboat

The spectacular sight of Spirit of Padstow launching down the slipway at Trevose Head, 2008. (By courtesy of Padstow RNLI)

Spirit of Padstow heads out after launching down the slipway at Trevose Head. (Nicholas Leach)

FIRST SERVICE OF 2018 • The first rescue of 2018 came on 8 January when Padstow lifeboat worked with and Newquay inshore lifeboat to assist a fishing boat which was disabled by a drifting trawl net and snagged on the seabed approximately four miles north west of Newquay. Newquay lifeboat crew were alerted just before 9.30am and launched the relief Atlantic 85 Martin Frederick Whitehouse to assist, with Padstow lifeboat putting out at around 9.45am. The 10m fishing boat with a father and son crew was hauling crab pots when its propeller and fishing gear became entangled in the net. A nearby fishing boat, crewed by one of Newquay's lifeboat volunteers, assisted with the tangled pots while Padstow lifeboat established a tow line. In light easterly winds and calm seas, Spirit of Padstow towed the fishing boat and her crew to the entrance of Newquay Harbour, where Newquay ILB took over and brought the boat safely in to the harbour. Newquay ILB returned to station at 12.30pm, three hours after launching, with Spirit of Padstow getting back to Trevose Head at 1.15pm after a routine incident.

and casualty awaiting favourable conditions over the bar. The injured casualty was transferred to the lifeboat and taken to Padstow station at Trevose Head. Two of the lifeboat crew stayed with the yacht and the remaining yacht crew while the helicopter stood by. On returning to the lifeboat station, the lifeboat crew assessed the casualty and handed her over to the ambulance crew. She was assessed by the ambulance crew, and no further treatment was needed.

The lifeboat launched again at 11.10pm and returned to the yacht, where a second member of the yacht's crew was found to be feeling cold and unwell, so was taken on board the lifeboat. The lifeboat crew then took the yacht under tow and, once the tide was high enough, and it was deemed safe to cross, the yacht was towed over the bar and safely into Padstow harbour. The Padstow crew at the station took the first casualty to the harbour, where she joined the rest of the yacht crew who were feeling better having come ashore. The lifeboat crew returned to the station at 4.45am after a very long service, having spent more tan seven hours at sea in north-easterly force six to seven winds. Coxswain Richard Pitman said :'It was a long night in challenging conditions, but there was great team work from our lifeboat crew and the Coastguard helicopter crew.'

Appendices

A • Lifeboat summary

Years on station (record)	Dimensions Type	Cost ON	Year built Builder	Name Donor

Hawker's Cove (known as No.1 1899–1938 and No.2 1938–62)

Years on station (record)	Dimensions / Type	Cost / ON	Year built / Builder	Name / Donor
1827 – 1856	23' x 6'6" Non-self-righter	£50 —	1827 Tredwen, Padstow	*Mariner's Friend* Local subscriptions and NSI funds
6.1856 – 1864 (9/38)	30' x 6' Peake self-righter	£133 —	1856 Forrestt, Limehouse	*Albert Edward* Local subscriptions and RNLI funds
6.1864 – 1883 (33/106)	32' x 7'4" Self-righter	£224 —	1864 Forrestt, Limehouse	*Albert Edward* City of Bristol Lifeboat Fund
8.1883 – 1900 (26/68)	34' x 8' Self-righter	£363 51	1883 Woolfe, Shadwell	*Arab* Gift of Mr R.A.B. Preston, London
1886 – 1887 (0/0)	33' x 8' Self-righter	£200 —	1863 Forrestt, Limehouse	*Elizabeth Moore Garden* [temp] Gift of late Mr R.T. Garden, Wicklow
9.1901 – 1931 (40/75)	36' x 8'3" Self-righter	£650 472	1901 Roberts, Mevagissey	*Arab* Gift of Mr R.A.B. Preston, London
1931 – 2.1938 (7/8)	35'6" x 8'10" Self-righter (M)	£3,754.9.5 743	1931 Saunders-Roe, Cowes	*John and Sarah Eliza Stych* Legacies of Mr and Mrs John Stych
2.1938 – 1939 (0/0)	34' x 8' Self-righter	£830 623	1911 Thames IW, Blackwall	*Docea Chapman* Legacy of Mr Joseph Chapman
1.1939 – 1947 (4/0)	35'6" x 8'10" Self-righter (M)	£3,821 738	1931 J. S. White, Cowes	*J. H. W.* Legacies of C. May, G.H.B. Haworth, E.F.S. Sackville, W. Johnson
1947 – 1951 (0/0)	35'6" x 8'10" Self-righter (M)	£3,742 747	1931 Saunders, Cowes	*Stanhope Smart* Legacy of Stanhope Smart, Huddersfield
7.1951–3.62 (13/6)	35'6" x 10'8" Liverpool (M)	£14,038 891	1951 Groves & Guttridge	*Bassett-Green* Gift of W. Bassett-Green, Winchcombe

Harbour (moored lifeboats)

Years on station (record)	Dimensions / Type	Cost / ON	Year built / Builder	Name / Donor
2.1899 – 4.1900 (4/9)	56'6" x 15'9" Steam	£3,340 421	1899 J. S. White, Cowes	*James Stevens No.4* Legacy of James Stevens, Birmingham
10.1901 – 1929 (19/10)	95'6" x 19'6" Steam tug	£9,784 478	1901 Ramage & Fergusun	*Helen Peele* Legacy of C. J. Peele, Chertsey
1901 – 7.1929 (41/78)	42' x 11'6" Self-righter	£1,351.7.5 475	1901 Thames IW, Blackwall	*Edmund Harvey* Gift of Mrs E. Harvey, London
25.5.1929 – 7.1952 (63/48)	61' x 15' Barnett (M)	£14,602 715	1929 S. E. Saunders, Cowes	*Princess Mary* P&O Shipping Companies
12.1952 – 11.1967 (91/15)	52' x 13'6" Barnett (M)	£31,584 898	1952 J. S. White, Cowes	*Joseph Hiram Chadwick* Legacy Miss E.E. Chadwick, Rochdale

Years on station (record)	Dimensions Type	Cost ON	Year built Builder	Name Donor

Trevose Head (slipway launched lifeboats)

Years on station (record)	Dimensions Type	Cost ON	Year built Builder	Name Donor
19.7.1967 – 6.1984 (109/63)	48'6" x 14' Oakley (M)	£53,000 989	1967 Berthon, Lymington	*James and Catherine MacFarlane* Gift of Mr Robert E. MacFarlane
7.1984 – 12.1984 (5/6)	52' x 14' x 6'10" Barnett (M)	£40,500 952	1960 Groves & Guttridge	*Duke of Cornwall (Civil Service No.33)* Civil Service Lifeboat Fund
12. 1984 – 7.2006	47' x 15' Tyne (M)	£451,906 1094	1984 Fairey Marine, Cowes	*James Burrough* Gift of Miss H. B. 'Mickie' Allen, Guildford
17.7.2006 –	16m x 5m Tamar (M)	£2,500,000 1283	2006 Green Marine/DML	*Spirit of Padstow* Gift of the late Miss H. B. 'Mickie' Allen

Rock (inshore lifeboats)

Years on station (record)	Dimensions Type	Cost ON	Year built Builder	Name Donor
26.3.1994 – 1995	16'3" x 6'7" D class inflatable	D-350	1987	— Legacy of Mrs Dorothy Martin
27.9.1995 – 2005	16'3" x 6'7" D class inflatable	D-489	1995 ILC, Cowes	*Dolly Holloway* Gift of Mr Michael Holloway
1.2.2005 – 2014	4.95m x 2m D class inflatable	£35,000 D-634	2005 ILC, Cowes	*Rusper* Gift of Mrs Anita Greenwood
6.10.2014 –	4.95m x 2m D class inflatable	D-772	2014 ILC, Cowes	*Rusper II* Gift of Pam Waugh aad Anita Greenwood

Spirit of Padstow on exercise, April 2011. (Nicholas Leach)

B • Moored and slipway lifeboats

James Stevens No.4

Official Number	421
On station	17 February 1899 – April 1900
Record	4 launches, 9 lives saved
Dimensions	56ft 6in x 15ft 9in x 5ft 8in
Type	Steam lifeboat
Engines	Compound steam engine and a patent water-tube boiler
Weight	31 tons 15 cwt
Built	J. S. White, Cowes, yard no. W1055
Donor	Legacy of Mr James Stevens, Birmingham
Cost	£3,340
Notes	Wrecked on service 11 April 1900 and subsequently broken up.

Helen Peele

Official Number	478
On station	11 September 1901 – 29 August 1917 and 17 April 1919 – May 1929 (taken over by Admiralty, with officers and crew, August 1917 – April 1919)
Record	19 launches, 10 lives saved (1901-17); 5 launches, 10 lives saved (1919-29)
Dimensions	95ft 6in x 19ft 6in x 11ft 6in
Type	Steam tug
Engines	Two compound engines driving twin screws, total 331ihp, running at 191rpm
Weight	133 tons
Built	Ramage & Fergusun, Leith
Donor	Legacy of Mr C. J. Peele, Chertsey.
Cost	£9,784 10s 0d
Notes	Sold out of service in May 1929 for £950 to Captain John Turner and was last reported as a yacht tender on the Clyde in 1964.

Edmund Harvey

Official Number	475
On station	September 1901 – July 1929
Record	41 launches, 78 lives saved
Dimensions	42ft x 11ft 6in x 5ft 6in
Type	Self-righter, twelve oars
Weight	8 tons 10 cwt
Built	Thames Iron Works, Blackwall, yard no. TI82
Donor	Gift of Mrs E. Harvey, London.
Cost	£1,351 7s 5d
Notes	Sold on 2 May 1929 for £70 and converted into the yacht *Trevone*, being fitted with a four-cylinder engine and based initially in the West Country. She moved about after the Second World War, and was re-engined several times. In the 1990s she was found at Faversham by French-based boatbuilder Simon Evans, who took her to his yard on the River Yonne at St Denis les Sens, France, and used her as a charter boat on the river for a number of years. Simon Evans owned a number of old lifeboats, and in about 2012 he moved them from St Denis les Sens to a boatyard at Migennes.

Princess Mary

Official Number	715
On station	25 May 1929 – July 1952
Record	63 launches, 48 lives saved
Dimensions	61ft x 15ft x 7ft 10in
Type	Barnett
Engines	Twin 80hp Weyburn-White DE.6 six-cylinder petrol
Weight	43 tons 10cwt
Built	S. E. Saunders, Cowes, yard no.S50
Donor	P and O Group of Shipping Companies.
Cost	£14,602 3s 0d
Notes	Sold out of service in June 1952 for £1,000 to Charles Harcourt-Smith, of London, who renamed her *Aries* and took her across the Atlantic; she was later used as a yacht, named *Aries B*, and kept at Saint-Jean-Cap-Ferrat, France.

Joseph Hiram Chadwick

Official Number	898
On station	December 1952 – November 1967
Record	91 launches, 15 lives saved
Dimensions	52ft x 13ft 6in
Type	Barnett
Engines	Twin 60hp Ferry VE.6 six-cylinder diesels to an RNLI design; re-engined in 1968 with twin 78hp Thornycroft 360 Mk.I Ford 2704E diesels
Weight	27 tons 9 cwt
Built	J. S. White, Cowes, yard no.W5427
Donor	Legacy of Miss Elizabeth Ellen Chadwick, Rochdale.
Cost	£31,583 13s 5d
Notes	Served at Galway Bay 1968-76 and in the Relief Fleet 1977-79. Sold out of service in April 1980 for £7,100 and renamed *Julia Clare*, then *Forceful*. She was kept on the south coast until the early 1990s, and then moved to Beccles, near Lowestoft.

James and Catherine Macfarlane

Official Number	989
On station	19 July 1967 – 9 October 1983
Record	109 launches, 63 lives saved
Dimensions	48ft 6in x 14ft
Type	Oakley self-righter, operational number 48-02
Engines	Twin 110hp Gardner 6LX six-cylinder diesels
Weight	31 tons 14 cwt
Built	Berthon Boat Company, Lymington
Donor	Gift of Mr Robert E. Macfarlane, of Glasgow, in memory of his father and mother.
Cost	£61,317 9s 1d
Notes	Served at The Lizard 1984-87 and taken out of service in 1988, to be loaned for display at the Land's End complex; in 2016 she was sold to a private owner.

Duke of Cornwall (Civil Service No.33)

Official Number	952
On station	31 July 1984 – 4 January 1985
Record	5 launches, 6 lives saved
Dimensions	52ft x 14ft x 6ft 10in
Type	Barnett
Engines	Twin 72hp Gardner 6LW six-cylinder diesels, speed nine knots
Weight	27 tons 11 cwt

Built	1960, Groves & Guttridge, Cowes, yard no.G&G 583
Donor	Civil Service Lifeboat Fund
Cost	£39,588 2s 5d
Notes	Served at Lizard-Cadgwith 1960-84 and in the Relief Fleet 1984-89; sold out of service in 1989 and kept by owners in Newcastle, Milford Haven and South Devon, remaining largely unaltered and named *Ex RNLB Duke of Cornwall*.

James Burrough

Official Number	1094
On station	28 December 1984 – 17 July 2006
Record	293 launches, 97 lives saved
Dimensions	47ft x 15ft
Type	Tyne, operational number 47-003
Engines	Twin 425hp General Motors 6V-92-TA diesels, speed eighteen knots
Weight	25 tons 5 cwt
Built	1984, Fairey Allday Marine, Cowes, yard no.FM 716
Donor	Gift of Miss H.B. 'Mickie' Allen, The Cottage, The Street, East Clandon, near Guildford, Surrey, in memory of her great-grandfather and as a tribute to the men of the lifeboat service.
Cost	£451,906
Notes	Sold 2007 to China Salvage & Rescue Bureau, renamed *Huaying 387*.

Spirit of Padstow

Official Number	1283
On station	17 July 2006 –
Dimensions	16m x 5m x 1.35m
Type	Tamar, operational number 16-04
Engines	Twin 1,015hp Cat C18 diesels, speed twenty-five knots
Weight	31.5 tonnes
Built	2005, hull by Green Marine, Lymington; fit out by DML, Devonport, yard no.065
Donor	Gift of the late Mis Mickie Allen.
Cost	£2,500,000
Notes	Named 17.9.2006 at North Quay, Padstow Harbour, by Peter Shone, friend of the late Mis Mickie Allen.

Relief 47ft Tyne Mariner's Friend (on left) with James Burrough off Appledore, circa 1990. Both lifeboats were funded by Miss Heather B. 'Mickie' Allen. (By courtesy of Padstow RNLI)

C • Service listing

Mariner's Friend Lifeboat

1833 Nov 29   Brig *Albion*, of London, saved 4

Albert Edward Lifeboat

1857 Mar 14   Schooner *Haberdine*, of Teignmouth, saved 4
1859 Mar 8   Brig *Gonsalve*, of Nantes, saved 7
       15   Schooner *Frederick William*, of Ipswich, saved 5
1861 Jan 1   Boat of schooner *Nugget*, of Bideford, saved 5
1862 Nov 9   Smack *Loftus*, of Padstow, saved 4
1863 Mar 18   Brigantine *Pandema*, of Plymouth, saved 8
       Schooner *Betsey*, of Brixham, saved 5

Albert Edward (second) Lifeboat

1864 Nov 26   Schooner *Elizabeth*, of Llanelly, assisted to
       safe moorings
       Lugger *Marie Estella*, of Nantes, assisted to
       safe moorings
1865 Dec 29   Barque *Juliet*, of Greenock, saved 17
1867 Dec 8   Smack *Telegraph*, of Padstow, saved 3
1868 Aug 22   Smack *Jules Josephine*, of Regneville, saved 4
       Oct 24   Steamship *Augusta*, of Bristole, assisted to save vessel
       and 6
1869 Jan 15   Brigantine *Thomas*, of Poole, saved 6
       Pilot gig, of Padstow, saved from above vessel 8
       Schooner *Alexandrine*, of Pornic, saved 6
       Sep 12   Lugger *Isabelle*, of Dinan, saved 4
1870 Jan 8   Barque *Suez*, saved 10
1872 Apr 2   Barque *Viking*, of Sunderland, saved 7
       Dec 27   Dandy *Caroline Phillips*, of Padstow, saved 3
1874 Nov 20   Schooner *Topaz*, of Glasgow, stood by
       29   Schooner *Huldah*, of Waterford, saved 5
       Dec 12   Brig *Thomas*, of Whitehaven, saved 6
       13   Brig *Thomas*, of Whitehaven, assisted to save
1875 Sep 26   Brigantine *Immacolata*, of Naples, saved 8
       Nov 6   Brig *Marie Josephine*, of Cherbourg, saved 4
1877 Feb 20   Schooner *Jeune Prosper*, saved 1
       Lugger *St Clement*, of Nantes, piloted to safety
       Schooner *Plymouth*, of Plymouth, saved 4
       Nov 24   Steamship *Ogmore*, of Hayle, stood by
1881 Oct 14   Schooner *Favourite*, of Quimpe, saved 4
       19   Trow *Two Brothers*, of Bridgwater, saved 3
       Dec 18   Barque *Milka*, of Fiume, stood by and gave help
1883 Feb 1   Schooner *Mary Josephine*, of Padstow, saved 3

Arab Lifeboat

1883 Sep 3   Schooner *Maria*, of Granville, saved 2
1884 Oct 10   Schooner *Eliza*, of Penzance, saved 5

Elizabeth Moore Garden Lifeboat
(from Bude, on temporary relief)

1886 Oct 17   Barque *Alliance*, of Risoer, saved 7

Arab Lifeboat
(returned after alterations)

1890 Jan 14   Ketch *Charles Francis*, of Plymouth, assisted to save
       vessel
       Nov 7   Brigantine *Helios*, of Tonsberg, saved 7
1892 Sep 29   Schooner *Madby Ann*, of London, saved 4
       Dec 24   Ketch *May Queen*, of Plymouth, landed 3 and assisted
       to save vessel

1894 Jan 13   Ketch *St Petroc*, of Padstow, rendered assistance
       Apr 24   Yawl *Oneida*, of Sennen Cove, saved yawl and 3
1895 Jan 2   Barque *Antoinette*, of St John NB, saved 4
       Barque *Antoinette*, of St John NB (second service),
       saved 5
       Feb 14   Ketch *Tavy*, of Plymouth, saved 4
       Mar 29   Schooner *Lizzie Trenberth*, of Fowey, stood by
       Oct 2   Ketch *William*, of Ipswich, saved 4
       3   Steamship *Sicilia*, of Liverpool, saved from a boat 16
1896 Oct 19   Lugger *Jules Noemi*, of Redon, saved 7
1897 Aug 31   Lugger *Boy George*, of Porthleven, assisted to save
1899 Apr 7   Ketch *Fairwater*, of Jersey, saved 4

Arab (second) Lifeboat

1903 Mar 1   Steam trawler *Binda*, of Milford, saved 9
       Steam trawler *Binda* (second service), assisted to save
       trawler
       Sep 6   Yacht *Shamrock*, of Padstow, assisted to save
1904 Feb 13   Trawler *Annie*, of Brixham, assisted to save 4
1905 Feb 20   Lifeboat *Edmund Harvey*, of Padstow (No.2), assisted
       to save Lifeboat
       Aug 3   Fishing yawl *Oneida*, of Sennen Cove, saved vessel
       and 3
1906 Jan 18   Schooner *Harvest Home*, of Preston, escorted
       Trawling ketch *Hadassah*, of Brixham, escorted
       Mar 19   Ketch *Selina Jane*, of Bristol, saved vessel and 3
1910 Feb 20   Trawler *New Boy*, of Lowestoft, stood by
       Aug 1   Schooner *Belle of the Plym*, of Padstow, stood by
1911 Feb 24   Trawler *Sunflower*, of Lowestoft, escorted vessel
       Trawler *Crimson Rose*, of Lowestoft, escorted
       Nov 12   Schooner *Island Maid*, of Belfast, saved 5
       Brigantine *Angele*, of Brest, saved 1
1913 May 4   Schooner *G. K. C.*, of Noirmontieres, assisted to save
       vessel and 6
1915 Feb 17   Steam drifter *True Friend*, of Lowestoft, assisted to save
       vessel and 9
1916 Feb 15   Trawler *Louisa*, of Ramsgate, assisted to save vessel
       and 4
       Apr 20   Ketch *Gem*, of Ramsgate, assisted to save vessel and 5
       Sep 19   Ketch *Endeavour*, of Ramsgate, saved 3
1917 Apr 26   Steamship *Heredia*, of Christiania, saved 5
       Aug 23   Steamship *Veghtstroom*, of Liverpool, landed 24
       Oct 4   Schooner *Colleen*, of Cork, saved 3
1918 Aug 25   Ketch *Republique et Patrie*, of Lorient, saved 4
1919 Jan 24   Ketch *Annie Ethel*, of Lowestoft, landed 5
1928 Feb 11   Steamship *Taormina*, of Oslo, saved 18

John and Sarah Eliza Stych Lifeboat

1933 Jan 4   Fishing boat, of Padstow, saved boat and 1
       July 9   Fishing boat May Flower, of St Ives, gave help
1935 Jan 24   Motor yacht *Martlet*, of Coews, gave help
       Sep 17   Ketch *Marie Celine*, of Drogheda, gave help
1936 Aug 6   Auxiliary cutter yacht *Vixen*, of Bude, saved 4
1938 Jan 19   Fishing boat *Rostellecois*, of Camaret, saved 3

Bassett-Green Lifeboat

1955 Sep 16   RAF Airborne Lifeboat, saved 5
1956 Oct 19   Dinghy *Betty*, of Padstow, saved boat and 1

No.2 Station

James Stevens No.4 Steam Lifeboat

1899	Apr 7	Brig *Emilie*, of Redon, assisted to save vessel and 7
	Dec 13	Fishing boat *Harriet Ann*, of Padstow, saved boat and 2

Edmund Harvey Lifeboat and *Helen Peele* steam tug

1901	Oct 6	(EH) Steam tug *Helen Peele*, of Padstow, assisted to refloat
	Dec 14-7	(EH+HP) Steamship *Auguste Legembre*, of Algiers, saved vessel and 30
1902	Dec 28	(EH+HP) Steamship *Baltazan*, of Sydney, saved 8
1903	Feb 22	(EH+HP) Steamship *Martha*, of Copenhagen, stood by
1908	Jan 8	(EH+HP) Barque *Europa*, of Oporto, saved 7
	Mar 6-7	(EH+HP) Steamship *Fjordheim*, of Oslo, saved vessel and 22
	Sep 1-2	(EH+HP) Ship *Talus*, of Greenock, stood by
	Dec 11-2	(EH+HP) Steamship *Martha*, of Horten, saved 7
1913	May 30	(EH) Fishing boat *Dreadnought*, of Padstow, saved boat and 1
	July 9	(HP) Steamship *Charlton*, of Andros, assisted to save vessel
1915	Jan 24-6	(HP) Steamship *Weehawken*, of Swansea, assisted to save vessel
	Mar 19	(EH+HP) Schooner *Francis*, of Lancaster, landed 5
	Oct 2	(EH+HP) Ketch *Trio*, of Guernsey, saved ketch and 4
	Dec 23	(HP) Schooner *Margaret Murray*, of Liverpool, assisted to save vessel
	28	(HP) Steamship *Taunton*, of Liverpool, saved vessel [with St Ives Lifeboat James Stevens No.10]
1916	Oct 29	(EH+HP) Trawling ketch Arethusa, of Lowestoft, saved 3
1917	Jun 29-30	(EH+HP) Trawling ketch *Pentire*, of Lowestoft, saved vessel
	July 7	(HP) Steamship *Rose Ann*, of Douglas, rendered assistance
	Dec-Jan 1919	(HP) Admiralty service as convoy rescue vessel, saved 11
1919	Sep 30	(EH+HP) HM Drifter *Crimson Rambler*, saved
	Dec 7	(HP) Schooner *Lord Devon*, of Salcombe, saved schooner and 5
1920	Mar 6-7	(EH+HP) Steamship *Bratton*, of Newcastle, saved
	Nov 1	(EH+HP) Motor schooner *Twee Ambt*, of Rotterdam, saved vessel
1921	Dec 1	(EH+HP) Fishing boat *Porpoise*, of Padstow, saved boat and 3
1928	Nov 27	(HP) Motor fishing boat *Our Girlie*, of Port Isaac, saved 5

Princess Mary Lifeboat

1930	Sep 19	Yacht *Emanuel*, of Bridgwater, saved yacht and 2
1933	Jan 30	Steamship *Cambalu*, of Liverpool, saved a ship's boat and 9
1934	July 29	Motor fishing boat *Only Two*, of Newquay, saved boat and 4
1938	Jan 24	Lighter OC.201, of Plymouth, saved lighter
1940	Jan 16	RAF Launch 101, escorted to harbour

Queen Victoria Reserve Lifeboat

1941	May 5	Motor vessel *Marie Flore*, of Antwerp, saved a ship's boat
		Motor vessel *Marie Flore*, of Antwerp (second service), assisted to save vessel

Princess Mary Lifeboat

1941	July 10	Steamship *Svint*, of Oslo, landed body and saved 10
1942	Dec 29	RAF air sea rescue launch, escorted launch
1944	Feb 17	Motor trawler *Atlantic*, of Ostend, saved vessel and 6
	Aug 9	HM Canadian ship *Regina* and steamship *Ezra Weston*, of Portland, Me, landed 4 and saved a boat
	Nov 23	Steamship *Sjofna*, of Oslo, saved 7
1946	Aug 17	Steamship *Kedah*, of Singapore, saved 10

Elsie Reserve Lifeboat

1946	Sep 12	Yacht *Diana III*, of Appledore, saved yacht and 2

Princess Mary Lifeboat

1947	Mar 29	Ex-Landing craft (M), of Falmouth, gave help
	May 11	Ex-RAF Tender, gave help
1950	June 17	RNAS Sea Otter seaplane, escorted to safety
1951	July 30	Motor yacht, of Bridgwater, gave help
1952	June 3	Fishing vessel *Willtoy*, of Fleetwood, gave help

Joseph Hiram Chadwick Lifeboat

1954	Nov 6	Motor yacht *Dawn Star*, of Cork, saved vessel
1955	May 28	Motor launch *Wave Hopper*, of Padstow, saved boat and 4
1956	Aug 19	Yacht *Isle of Rona*, gave help
1957	Dec 8-9	Motor vessel *Tubo*, of Delfzijl, escorted vessel

Lloyds Reserve Lifeboat

1958	Jan 10	RNLB *Bassett-Green*, of Padstow, saved boat and 7

Joseph Hiram Chadwick Lifeboat

1958	May 16	Motor vessel *Musketeer*, of Groningen, stood by
	Aug 29	Motor boat St Minver, of Padstow, gave help
1959	June 17	Motor boat *Susan Ann*, of Padstow, saved boat and 3
	Oct 1	Motor launch *Empress of England*, gave help
1960	Aug 8	Recovered a body from the sea off Trevose Lighthouse
	16	Sailing dinghy, saved dinghy and 1
1961	Jan 12	Fishing boat *Moonlit Waters*, of Padstow, landed 1
	13	Motor fishing boat *Moonlit Waters*, of Padstow, escorted vessel to harbour
	Aug 16	Motor boat *Good Intent*, saved boat and 1
1962	May 3	Sailing dinghy, of Newquay, landed 2, saved boat
	Aug 17	Persons cut off by tide, stood by for cliff rescue
	Dec 1	Motor vessel *Nimrod*, of Groningen, stood by
1963	Nov 16	Fishing boat *Dawn*, of Port Isaac, escorted
1964	Jul 18	Yacht *Daphne Loo*, of Gloucester, saved yacht and 3
	Sep 9	Motor boat, saved boat and 2
1965	Mar 3	Belgian trawler *Sanatonias*, took out doctor
	Jun 15	Yacht *Sea Ranger*, escorted yacht
	Nov 23	Fishing boat *Deo Gratias*, of Barnstaple, saved 2
1966	Feb 26	Steam trawler *Combesco*, of Ostend, escorted
	May 27	Motor yacht *Ranger of Lune*, of Glasgow, gave help
1967	Apr 1	Cabin cruiser *Vigilante*, gave help
	Jul 22	Yacht *Santos*, escorted yacht
	Sep 20	Newquay inshore lifeboat, gave help
	Oct 18	Fishing boat *Elaner Ann*, saved boat and 2

Trevose Head Station

James and Caherine Macfarlane Lifeboat

1968	Aug 21	Motor boat *Spes*, saved boat (also a dog) and 6
1969	Jan 19	Man fallen from cliff, landed a body
	May 2	Yacht *Rosemary*, saved yacht and 2
	12	Steam tanker *Hemsley I*, of London, stood by
	Jul 7	Ketch yacht *Minoru*, of Fleetwood, saved yacht and 5
	Aug 22	Motor cruiser *Mervic*, saved yacht and 4
1970	Aug 1	Ketch yacht *Kilo*, gave help
1971	Jun 18	Fishing boat *Elaner Ann*, of Milford, escorted
	Sep 6	Fishing boat *Blue Shark*, saved boat and 8
	Nov 30	Motor vessel *Olna Firth*, of Newcastle, stood by
1972	May 1	Trimaran *Kemar*, gave help
	25	Yacht *Merillisa*, stood by
	Dec 27	Tanker *British Seafarer*, of London, landed a sick man, saving 1
1973	Feb 22	Motor tug Plastron, of London, landed 3 and a body
	27	Belgian trawler *Apollo*, landed a sick man
	Jul 31	Fishing boat *Christine*, of Padstow saved boat and 2

Gertrude Relief Lifeboat

1974	Aug 24	Fishing boat *Boy Steve*, gave help
	Sep 2	Injured man on board fishing boat *Twilight*, of Belgium, took out doctor
	Oct 10	Cabin cruiser *Melamine*, escorted

James and Caherine Macfarlane Lifeboat

1975	Jan 31	Fishing boat *Kreisker*, of Milford, escorted
	Feb 9	Fishing boat *St Stanislas*, of Padstow, gave help
	10	Fishing boat *Twilight*, landed an injured man
	Apr 7	Motor fishing vessel *Elizabeth Ann Webster*, of Brixham, saved vessel and 6
	29	Fishing boat *Jean Pierre Andre*, escorted
	Jul 19	Yacht *Jesmond II*, gave help
	Sep 9	Motor launch *Sea Cat*, escorted
	Oct 11	Sand dredger *Sir Cedric*, saved vessel and 3

Gertrude Relief Lifeboat

	Dec 13	Fishing boat *Reina Dee*, escorted
1976	Jan 3	Motor vessel *Ekenis*, stood by

James and Caherine Macfarlane Lifeboat

	Feb 14	Motor trawler *Bryher*, of Lowestoft, gave help
	Mar 15	Trawler *Okeanos*, of OStaend, landed an injured man
	Apr 9	Trawler *Nautilus*, of Belgium, landed a sick man
	July 12	Motor trawler *L'Aange Gardien*, of Falmouth, saved vessel and 2
	31	Yacht *Panacea*, of Milford, gave help
1977	July 17	Yacht *Calcutta Princess*, saved yacht and (also a dog) 2
	Aug 25	Yacht *Calcutta Princess*, saved yacht and (also a dog) 1
	28	Sailing surf board, gave help
	Dec 27	Yacht *Freedom*, saved 1
1978	Jan 23	Trawler *Coudekercke*, of Belgium, landed injured man

Gertrude Relief Lifeboat

	July 21	Yacht *Gay Salar*, of Weymouth, escorted yacht
	Aug 1	Yacht *Golden Leigh*, of Dun Laoghaire, took doctor to three injured persons on bd & esc yt
	Nov 5	Fishing boat *Roma*, of Newquay, saved boat and 3

James and Caherine Macfarlane Lifeboat

1979	May 15	Fishing boat *Girl Anne*, of Padstow, saved boat and 3
	July 1	Cabin cruiser *Gay Dawn*, of London, gave help
	Aug 10	Motor vessel *River Taw*, of Barnstaple, stood by

	14	Yacht *Thomasin II*, took doctor to sick man, escorted
	Aug 14	Trawler *Petit Poisson*, of France, gave help
		Yacht *Tarantula*, saved yacht and landed 1
		Yacht *Mosika Alma*, gave help
	15	Catamaran *Palnklina*, saved craft and 3
	Sep 3	Yacht *Peggy*, saved yacht and 9
	Dec 15	Motor vessel *Skopelos Sky*, of Piraeus, stood by
1980	Jan 19	Motor fishing vessel *Venturer*, gave help

Gertrude Relief Lifeboat

	Feb 14	Trawler *Kalos*, took out doctor, landed injured man
	Mar 26	Fishing boat *Aaltje Adriaan*, of Penzance, took out doctor and landed an injured man
	May 5	Trawler *Goeland*, saved vessel

James and Caherine Macfarlane Lifeboat

	Oct 16	Fishing boat *Girl Christian*, of Newquay, in tow of fishing bt Minehead Angler, escorted
1981	Sep 8	Yacht *Madcap*, gave help
	Oct 2	Yacht *Spray of Avon*, of Bristol, saved boat and 4
		Yacht *Argo*, escorted boat
1982	Jan 5	Fishing vessel *Camelot Challenger*, of Padstow, recovered wreckage
	26	Fishing vessel *Lamorna*, of Padstow, gave help
	Mar 27	Fishing vessel *Treryn Castle*, of Padstow, gave help
		Fishing vessel *St Agnes*, escorted vessel and landed 3
	June 28	Yacht *July Morn*, escorted boat
	Aug 6	Yacht *UFO*, of Douglas, gave help
1983	May 1	Yacht *Starfisher*, of Swansea, saved boat and 1
	Aug 26	Yacht, gave help
		Port Isaac Inshore Lifeboat, gave help

Guy and Clare Hunter Lifeboat

1984	May 22	Trawler *Lesley Elizabeth*, of Brixham, gave help
		Trawler *Charmaine M*, gave help
	31	Motor cruiser *Jersey Wanderer*, saved boat and 3

Duke of Cornwall (C. S. No.33) Lifeboat

	July 29	Skin diver, gave help
	Oct 21	Yacht *Talahinna*, of Littlehampton, saved boat and 6

James Burrough Lifeboat

1985	Feb 20	Fishing vessel *Lady Joanna*, of Maryport, gave help
	July 27	Salvage vessel *Torfness*, gave help
	Aug 2	Injured man on board fishing vessel *Jean Marc*, took out doctor and landed an injured man
		Yacht *Seagoe*, saved boat and 6
	13	Fishing vessel *Shiela Pat*, in tow of fishing vessel *Ju-El*, escorted
	Sep 20	Sick man on board cargo vessel *Malling*, took our doctor and landed a sick man
	Nov 14	Motor fishing vessel *Can Far Ien*, escorted vessel
1986	Mar 9	Survivors of fishing vessel *Ocean Harvest*, of Brixham, on board fishing vessel *Dolly Mop*, landed 3
	Apr 11	Yacht *Seagoe*, saved 6
	14	Sick boy on board fishing vessel *Tannetje*, of Brixham, took out doctor and escorted vessel
1987	Jan 12	Cargo vessel *Mare*, of Honduras, escorted vessel
	Apr 20	Fishing vessel *Ross Alcedo*, of Panama, gave help
	July 8	Fishing vessel *Invicta*, of Penzance, gave help
	Sep 23	Fishing vessel *L.M.A.*, of St Ives, saved vessel and 3
	Oct 21	Yacht *Arbrook*, saved boat and 2
1988	Jan 10	Fishing vessel *Laura Jane*, of Padstow, recovered a body and wreckage
	11	Fishing vessel *Laura Jane*, recovered wreckage
	Feb 12	Cargo vessel *Westland*, of Cyprus, gave help

Sam and Joan Woods Relief Lifeboat

	May	3	Fishing vessel *Osprey*, gave help
	July	2	Inshore lifeboat D-366, of Port Isaac, escorted boat
		31	Fishing vessel *Lucky Star*, gave help
	Aug	8	Fishing vessel *L'Aurore*, gave help
		28	Catamaran *Tikaroa*, saved boat (also a cat) and 3
	Sep	10	Two skin divers, landed 2
		24	Two sailboards, saved two boards and 2

James Burrough Lifeboat

1989	Mar	12	Sailboard, saved board
			Cargo vessel *Secil Japan*, stood by
		16	Yacht *Eugene Marie*, saved boat and 2
	Apr	3	Injured man on board fishing vessel *Emerald Star*, landed an injured man
	June	4	Dinghy, saved 1
	July	26	Yacht *Christina*, stood by
	Nov	19	Fishing vessel *Carhelmar*, gave help
	Dec	15	Fishing vessel *Princess*, gave help
1990	Feb	21	Fishing vessels, stood by
	Mar	15	Fishing vessel *Sea Image*, in tow of fishing vessel *Ariedirk*, gave help
		22	Sick man on board fishing vessel *Admiral Gordon*, landed a sick man
			Fishing vessel *Admiral Gordon*, gave help
	Apr	8	Cabin cruiser *Boy James*, saved boat and 2
		16	Yacht *Dasler*, saved boat and 4
	May	8	Fishing vessel *Four Sisters*, gave help
	June	11	Yacht *Exhaven*, saved boat and 2
	Sep	3	Sailboard, saved board and 1
	Oct	12	Fishing vessel *Admiral Blake*, gave help
1991	Jan	11	Cabin cruiser *Reef Diver*, saved boat and 2
		15	Sick man on board fishing vessel *Admiral Blake*, landed a sick man
		26	Fishing vessel *Blaidd*, gave help
	Mar	2	Injured man on board fishing vessel *Heather Lea II*, landed an injured man
		4	Fishing vessel *Lady Sylvia*, recovered wreckage
			Fishing vessels *Ariedirk* and *Try Again*, escorted vessel
	May	27	Cabin cruiser *Super Trouper*, gave help
	July	10	Fishing vessel *Kael Coz*, saved 4
		19	Motor boat, landed 2 and saved boat
			Two yachts, escorted boats
	Aug	12	Cabin cruiser *Super Tramp*, saved boat and 2
		13	Cabin cruiser *Super Tramp*, gave help
	Sep	21	Fishing vessel *Pearn Pride*, landed 3
		29	Three sailboards, saved 1 board

Mariner's Friend Relief Lifeboat

| | Dec | 7 | Fishing vessel *Our Zoe Anne*, took out fire personnel and escorted vessel |
| 1992 | Jan | 7 | Fishing vessel *Dummonia*, gave help |

James Burrough Lifeboat

	Jan	19	Fishing vessel *Nils Desperandum*, gave help
	Mar	16	Fishing vessel *Rose In June*, saved 3
	Apr	12	Yacht *Rosina*, escorted boat
		18	Yacht *Accushnet*, escorted boat
		24	Yacht *Melyn Trefin*, saved boat and 2
		25	Yacht *Pieta*, escorted boat
		30	Motor cruiser *Robin Hood*, in tow of fishing vessel *Lady Helen*, gave help
	May	17	Sailing dinghy, gave help
	June	8	Dinghy, landed 2 and saved boat
		18	Yacht *Zebedee*, saved boat and 2

	July	5	Yacht *Playmate*, gave help
			Sailboard, saved board
			Sailboard, saved board and 1
		11	Yacht *Jenami*, gave help
		19	Injured man on board fishing vessel *George William C*, landed an injured man
	Aug	1	Yacht *Fearnought*, gave help
			Yacht *Fulmarus*, gave help
		15	Yacht *Misty Blue*, gave help
		16	Motor cruiser *Sun Bird III*, gave help
	Sep	3	Yacht *Karm*, escorted
		21	Motor launch, in tow of tug *Glen Husk*, gave help
		22	Fishing vessel *Phra-Nang*, escorted vessel
	Nov	29	Sick man on board fishing vessel *Morning Dawn*, landed a sick person
	Dec	21	Fishing vessel *Heather Lea II*, gave help
		24	Body in sea, landed a body
1993	Feb	27	Yacht *Meander*, saved boat and 2
	Mar	14	Man fallen from cliff, recovered a body
		23	Fishing vessel *Bois Rosie*, saved vessel and 7

Mariner's Friend Relief Lifeboat

| | | 31 | Fishing vessel *Admiral Blake*, escorted vessel |
| | Apr | 4 | Yacht *Myth of Skye*, saved boat and 2 |

James Burrough Lifeboat

	May	12	Sick man on board yacht *Orm Fox*, took out doctor and escorted boat
			Helicopter winchman, gave help
	June	12	Yacht *Viking Lass VII*, gave help
	July	19	Minesweeper *Margherita*, escorted boat
	Aug	22	Sailboard, saved board and 1
			Sailboard, recovered sail
		27	Punt, gave help
		29	Yacht *Penguin*, gave help
	Sep	7	Motor cruiser *Our Michelle*, escorted boat
		19	Sailboard, gave help
	Oct	4	Yacht *Citara III*, gave help
1994	Feb	2	Fishing vessel *Wendy Pulfrey*, escorted vessel
	Apr	29	Cabin cruiser *Lady Monaco*, gave help
	June	28	Motor cruiser *Avanti*, two persons and craft brought in saved by another lifeboat
	July	6	Yacht *Flight*, assisted to save boat and 1
	Aug	7	Punt *Lucky Lad*, four persons and craft brought in
		10	Punt, saved boat and 2
	Sep	3	Fishing vessel *Sparfell*, two persons and craft brought in
		14	Canoe, saved boat and 2
	Nov	23	Fishing vessel *Chrisande*, landed 4
1995	Jan	25	Fishing vessel *L.M.A.*, saved 2
		31	Surfboard, saved board and 1
	Mar	11	Fishing vessel *Su-Jean*, landed 3 and craft brought in
		26	Fishing vessel *L. & T. Britannia V*, landed 5 and craft brought in
	Apr	15	Cabin cruiser *Sinaloa*, escorted boat
		16	Motor boat *Yellow Custard*, saved boat
	May	4	Fishing vessel *Batara Star*, saved vessel and 5
	June	2	Trimaran *Quantum Leap*, saved boat and 2
		16	Yacht *Mistrim*, two persons and craft brought in
		21	Cabin cruiser *Sea Jay VI*, landed 3 & craft brought in
	July	14	Tug *Wilpower*, landed 6 and craft brought in
	Aug	12	Yacht *Red Witch*, landed 3 and craft brought in
		20	Body in sea, landed a body
		22	Trimaran *Swift Promise*, landed 4 and craft brought in
		31	Yacht *Tobyruf*, two persons and craft brought in
	Sep	18	Yacht *Larus*, landed 2 and craft brought in

	Dec 3	Motor cruiser *Searaker*, saved boat and 3
1996	Jan 13	Fishing vessel *Try Again*, saved vessel and 5
	Feb 4	Fishing vessel *Provider*, two persons & craft brought in

Owen and Ann Aisher Relief Lifeboat

Feb 28   Fishing vessel *Oneida*, two persons & craft brought in

James Burrough Lifeboat

June	6	Catamaran *Manu Maonu*, escorted craft
July	27	Yacht *Baraka*, two persons and craft brought in
	28	Motor launch *Signal*, saved craft and 3
	29	Yacht *Sea Jay*, two persons and craft brought in
	30	Yacht *Arenys*, five persons and craft brought in
Aug	6	Yacht *Brandy Snap*, escorted craft
Sep	9	Motor cruiser *Inis-Ealga II*, five persons and craft brought in
Nov	17	Trimaran *Jake the Peg*, three persons & craft brought in

Voluntary Worker Relief Lifeboat

	Dec 14	Injured man onboard fishing vessel *Espadon Bleu*, injured man brought in
1997	Feb 9	Motor boat *Jim Bobb*, landed a body
	Mar 17	Fishing vessel *St Antonius*, four persons and craft brought in
	20	Sick man on board fishing vessel *Our Emma Jo*, landed a sick man
	21	Fishing vessel *Don Bosco*, four persons and craft brought in

James Burrough Lifeboat

May	7	Yacht *Manny III*, two persons and craft brought in
July	15	Yacht *Kittyflo II*, saved craft and 3
Aug	12	Yacht *Sunbeam*, gave help
	14	Yacht *True Blue*, one person and craft brought in
	23	Yacht *Sea Bear*, assisted to save craft

Ruby and Arthur Reed II Relief Lifeboat

Sep 20   Catamaran *Koh-I-Noor*, landed 2 and craft brought in

James Burrough Lifeboat

1998	May 1	Yacht *Bllion*, landed 2 and craft brought in
		Youth fallen over cliffs at *Ocean View* caravan park, assisted to save 1
	12	Sick man on board fishing vessel *Arrivain II*, landed a sick man
June	21	Fishing vessel *Coral Anne*, three persons and craft brought in
July	22	Yacht *Arenys*, landed 3 and craft brought in
Aug	10	Motor cruiser *Horizon*, two persons & craft brought in
Sep	6	Man and boy trapped in cave at Bossinney, gave help Inflatable lifeboat D-517, of Port Isaac, assisted to save 1
	15	Yacht *Meoldy*, one person and craft brought in
Oct	5	Yacht *Little Island*, saved caft and 2
1999	Feb 4	Fishing vessel *Jannie Marie*, five persons and craft brought in
	Apr 3	Fishing vessel *Hawkwind*, two persons and craft brought in
	30	Yacht *Kes*, saved craft and 2

Owen and Anne Aisher Relief Lifeboat

June 9   Fishing vessel *Iris III*, two persons and craft brought in

James Burrough Lifeboat

Aug	31	Yacht *Wind Thief*, gave help
Sep	6	Fishing vessel *Defiant*, saved craft and 5
Oct	30	Fishing vessel *Charisma*, five persons & craft brought in

2000	Mar 31	Fishing vessel *Su Jean*, stood by
	May 19	Yacht *cassiopeia*, two persons and craft brought in
	June 10	Sailboard, saved 1
	13	Powerboat *Amerella*, escorted craft
	18	Inshore lifeboat *Spirit of the PCS RE II*, of Port Isaac, four persons and craft brought in
	Aug 1	Yacht *Myansa*, two persons and craft brought in
	Oct 10	Fishing vessel *Defiant*, gave help
	Dec 1	Fishing vessel *Jannie Marie*, saved craft and 3
	2	Fishing vessel *Silver Harvester*, landed 6 and craft brought in
2001	Jan 14	Fishing vessel *Admiral Gordon*, gave help
	Mar 11	Yacht *Schiemallion*, landed 2 and craft brought in
	Apr 8	Powerboats *NT Free* and *Eivado*, escorted craft
	May 8	Yacht *Scatter Cash*, landed 1 and craft brought in
	11	Yacht *Cassiopeiao*, two persons and craft brought in Yacht *Tambourine*, one person and craft brought in
	12	Yacht *Sluma*, four persons and craft brought in
	29	Fishing vessel *Challenger*, one person & craft brought in
	30	Fishing vessel *Oyserhound*, two persons and craft brought in
	June 16	Ex Thames fireboat *Firebrace*, saved craft and 2
	July 14	Yacht *Hideaway*, escorted craft
	17	Yacht *Su-Ka-Dee*, landed 2 and craft brought in
	Aug 4	Sailboard, saved craft and 1
	31	Catamaran *Wildwind*, landed 1
	Sep 7	Fishing vessel *Arthur Biff*, assisted to save craft and 1
	Oct 12	Recovery of human remains, landed a body
	Nov 11	Fishing vessel *Daymer Bay*, two persons and craft brought in
	25	Yacht *Kyra*, escorted craft
	Dec 12	Fishing trawler *Helen Jane*, two and craft brought in
2002	Mar 29	Motor cruiser *Molly Odwyer*, five persons and craft brought in
	June 2	Yacht *Snow White*, two persons and craft brought in
	11	Yacht *Jenos*, landed 1 and craft brought in
	July 10	Cabin cruiser *Holly Rose*, three persons and craft brought in
	11	Person in danger of drowning, saved 1
	26	Motor cruiser *Seaclusion*, two persons and craft brought in
	Aug 8	Yacht *Brynmawr*, landed 2 and craft brought in
	Oct 1	Yacht *Wild Raven*, two persons and craft brought in
	2	Motor boat *Dabbler*, gave help

Sarah Emily Harrop Relief Lifeboat

Nov	27	Fishing vessel *Pieter*, six persons and craft brought in
Dec	19	Merchant vessel *Sena Deniz*, gave help

James Burrough Lifeboat

2003 May 21   Yacht *Snow Goose*, one person and craft brought in

Sarah Emily Harrop Relief Lifeboat

May	24	Fishing vessel *Helen Jane II*, escorted craft
June	13	Cabin cruiser *Pipe Dream*, two persons and craft brought in
	22	Cabin cruiser *Metro Gnome*, escorted vessel
	29	Yacht *Levington Lass*, two persons and craft brought in

James Burrough Lifeboat

July	26	Fishing vessel *Band of Hope*, two persons and craft brought in
Sep	1	Yacht *Puddleduck*, two persons and craft brought in Motor vessel *Lady In Red*, two persons and craft brought in

	Oct 10	Fishing vessel *Lilly-L*, gave help
	31	Person in the water, assisted to save 1
	Dec 9	Fishing vessel *Tigger*, escorted craft
2004	Jan 15	Fishing vessel *Charisma*, one person brought in
	Feb 14	Fishing vessel *Neptune*, two persons & craft brought in
	Mar 31	Angling vessel *Lady Mary II*, two persons and craft brought in
	May 29	Angling vessel *Batara Star*, landed 2 & craft brought in
	July 29	Yacht *Celtic Gourmet*, two persons and craft brought in
	Aug 7	Sailing dinghy, craft brought in
	14	Fishing vessel *Three Gees*, craft brought in
	17	Flooding at Boscastle, saved one craft
	Sep 15	Liferaft, craft brought in
	24	Catamaran *Kittywakes 3*, five persons and craft brought in
		Yacht *Spirata*, gave help
	27	Fishing vessel *Helen Jane I*, two persons and craft brought in
2005	Feb 19	Fishing vessel *Francis of Ladram*, gave help – passed tow to Sennen Cove lifeboat
	Apr 19	Sick man on board yacht *L'Enfant de Mer*, gave help
	June 14	Yacht *Simply Red*, escorted craft
	July 19	Yacht *Plover*, one person and craft brought in
	Oct 4	Fishing vessel *Keriolet*, three persons & craft brought in
	20	Fishing vessel *Intuition*, seven persons and craft brought in
	22	Fishing vessel *Intuition*, seven persons and craft brought in
		Fishing vessel *Diligence*, three persons and craft brought in
	Nov 8	Yacht *Rionnag*, two persons and craft brought in
2006	Jan 27	Powered boat *Diadem*, three persons & craft brought in
	Feb 14	Work boat *Pont Menai*, three persons and craft brought in
	22	Fishing vessel *Kerloch*, six persons and craft brought in
	26	Fishing vessel *Kerloch*, gave help – laid anchor
		Fishing vessel *Kerloch*, six persons and craft brought in
	May 28	Fishing vessel *Trevose*, three persons & craft brought in
	June 4	Yacht *Finesse*, two persons brought in, one assisted and craft brought in
	8	Yacht *Eleonora*, two persons and craft brought in
	18	Yacht *Jessie Williams*, two persons and craft brought in
	24	Powered boat *Havilar*, three persons & craft brought in
	July 12	Yacht *Avianta*, four persons and craft brought in

Spirit of Padstow Lifeboat

	Aug 5	Powered boat *Henneke*, three persons and craft brought in

Peter and Lesley-Jane Nicholson Relief

	25	Yacht *Incus*, one person and craft brought in

Spirit of Padstow Lifeboat

	Sep 18	Yacht *Niveus*, two persons and craft brought in
	Oct 8	Yacht *Sea Itch*, two persons and craft brought in
	Dec 20	Powered boat *Classic Lines*, gave help
2007	Jan 26	Fishing vessel *Eclipse*, one person and craft brought in
	Apr 30	Yacht *Synergy*, five people and craft brought in
	May 6	Yacht *Hara*, two people and craft brought in
	9	Yacht *Turin Lady*, escorted craft
	16	Fishing vessel *Golden Harvest*, four people and craft brought in
	June 9	Yacht *Standancer*, three people and craft brought in
	11	Survey vessel *Ile de Brehat*, landed 1
	25	Yacht *Coresande*, saved craft
		Yacht *Fly*, saved 1

	July 2	Swimmers trapped in cave, saved 1
	15	Fishing vessel *Salamander*, three people and craft brought in
	22	Powered boat *Lazy Dreamer*, one craft brought in
	Aug 3	Powered boat *Anneca*, one person & craft brought in
	Sep 14	Yacht *Xenon*, three people and craft brought in
	18	Fishing vessel *Trevose*, three people and craft brought in
	Oct 26	Fishing vessel *Helen-Jane*, two people and craft brought in
	Nov 22	Powered boat *Alcatraz*, escorted craft
2008	Apr 10	Fishing vessel *Icthus*, four people and craft brought in
	May 2	Yacht *Supersonic*, three people and craft brought in
	July 1	Yacht *Salamander*, three people and craft brought in
	22	Fishing vessel *Viking*, two people and craft brought in
	30	Yacht *Sparky*, landed 4 and craft brought in
	Aug 7	Powered boat *Mystery*, two people & craft brought in
	17	Powered boat, one person and craft brought in
	18	Fishing vessel *Thomas Andrew*, stood by
	26	Powered boat *Miss Bovril*, gave help – took over tow from Bude lifeboat
	27	Yacht *Olli*, three people and craft brought in
	Sep 5	Yacht *Freya*, two people and craft brought in
	6	Yacht *Freya*, gave help
	12	Person in the sea, gave help
	20	Angling vessel *Batara Star 2*, four people and craft brought in
2009	Jan 26	Kiteboard, saved 1

Frank and Anne Wilkinson Relief Lifeboat

	Apr 12	Kayak, one person and craft brought in
	June 6	Yacht *Stargate*, four people and craft brought in

Spirit of Padstow Lifeboat

	Aug 8	Dog, gave help
	10	Yacht *Kalyptos*, three people and craft brought in
	11	Yacht *Escapade of France*, two people & craft brought in
	25	Yacht *Maui*, gave help
		Yacht *Carol of Bosham*, two people & craft brought in
	Sep 18	Fishing vessel *Northern Lights*, three people and craft brought in
	25	Fishing vessel *Tizardlyon*, stood by
	Oct 1	Fishing vessel *Amber Mist*, escorted craft

Frank and Anne Wilkinson Relief Lifeboat

	25	Tug *DMS World*, escorted craft

Spirit of Padstow Lifeboat

2010	Apr 15	Powered boat *Jessica Rose*, three people and craft brought in
	June 14	Sick people on board yacht *Arkadina*, landed 2 and craft brought in
	Aug 5	Injured man on fishing vessel *Band of Hope*, landed 1
	16	Powered boat *Maura B*, two people & craft brought in
	Sep 3	Fishing vessel *Tiz Ardly On*, gave help – freed craft
	13	Fishing vessel *Trevose*, three people & craft brought in
	18	Powered boat *La Mor*, two people & craft brought in
	Nov 25	Injured man on tug *Indus*, landed 1
2011	Apr 2	Dog fallen over cliff, gave help
	28	Yacht *Elsker*, two people and craft brought in
	29	Yacht *Watersmeet*, two people and craft brought in
	July 11	Yacht, craft brought in
	20	Fishing vessel *Chantelle*, escorted
	Aug 5	Yacht *Granvelle*, craft brought in
	15	Fishing vessel *Serene Dawn*, craft brought in
	27	Yacht *Granvelle*, one person and craft brought in

D • Personnel summary

Honorary Secretary*

Rev Richard Tyacke	1856 – 1881
Robert B. Key	1882 – 1887
W. Martyn Richards	1888 – 1895
R. Sussex Langford	1895 – 1895
William H. Pope	1895 – 1903
F. Harvey	1904 – 1910
Richard Binny	1910 – 1923
E. P. Hutchings	1924 – 1933
E. Bluett	1934 – 1937
R. R. Wilton	1937 – 1962
Frank J. Andrews	1962 – 1963
A. G. Trembath	1963 – 1969
L. S. Marchant	1969 – 1970
Harry H. Lobb	1970 – 1978
James Hamilton	1978 – 1983
Frank Sluman	1983 – 1984
H. Trevor Ramsden	1984 – 1989
Ralph H. Chalker	1989 – 1991
George C. Phillips	1991 – 2002
Michael Walker	2002 – 2006
Captain Trevor Platt	2006 – 2016
Martin Biddle	2016 –

*Title changed to Lifeboat Operations Manager in 2002

Martin Bddle has been Lifeboat Operations Manager since 2016.

Coxswain

Daniel Shea	1857 – 1862
William Hills	1862 – 1870
William Cockhill	1870 – 1875
William Webb	1875 – 1883
Samuel Philp	1883 – 1885
Thomas Henry Edyvane	1885 – 1892
David Grubb	1892 – 1899
Samuel Brown	1899 – 1904
William Henry Baker	1904 – 1923
William John Baker	1924 – 1948
Horace Bernard Murt	1948 – 1962

Helen Peele (steam tug)

Capt H. H. Stribley	1901 – 1908
Capt A. Mitchell	1908 – 1916
Capt F. Andrew	1916 – 1923
Capt J. Atkinson	1923 – 1929

Afloat/Trevose Head lifeboats

David Grubb	1899 – 1900
William Henry Baker	1901 – 1902
Edward Oldham	1902 – 1922
Herbert Brown	1922 – 1929
Joe Atkinson	1929 – 1944
John Tallack Murt	1944 – 1964
Gordon Harvey Elliott	1964 – 1971
Anthony William Warnock	1972 – 1978
Trevor Raymond England	1978 – 1993
Alan Clive Tarby	1993 – 2016
Richard Pitman	2016 –

Mechanic

William Orchard	1931 – 1933
Percy Baker	1933 – 1962
Arthur Banham	1929 – 1935
J. Rokaber	1935 – 1948
W. F. Phillips	1950 – 1953
William Bray	1954 – 1960
George Pinch	1961 – 1970
E. Pearson	1970 – 1971
Horace Edward Murt	1971 – 1988
John Alldridge	1988 – 2004
Michael England	2004 –

Padstow Lifeboat Personnel 2018

Coxswain Richard Pitman joined the crew in July 1984. A fisherman and then plant operator, he was Second Coxswain prior to his appointment as Coxswain in October 2016.

Mechanic Mike England joined the crew in 1987, became the station's full-time mechanic in May 2004, and Second Coxswain in 2017.

Second Mechanic Michael Smith joined the crew in 1992. He works as the foreman for Padstow Harbour Commissoners.

Deputy Second Coxswain James Chown joined the crew in October 1997; he is a fisherman who skippers his own boat out of Newlyn.

Padstow lifeboat personnel

Top left • George Pinch served as the station's Mechanic from 1961 to 1970 having previously been a Fleet Mechanic with the RNLI.

Top right • John Tallack Murt was Coxswain from 1944 to 1964 and was awarded the Silver medal for the rescue of the steamship Kedah.

Middle left • Tony Warnock served as Coxswain from 1971 to 1978. He had previously been a travelling mechanic, stationed at Seahouses and Spurn.

Middle right • Second Coxswain Donnie McBurnie, on the crew from 1954 to 1968, in the wheelhouse of James and Catherine Macfarlane with Gordon Elliot (Coxswain 1964-1971) and Mechanic George Pinch.

Left • Edward Murt was Mechanic from 1971 to 1988 having joined the crew in 1948. He was also awarded the British Empire Medal.

Top left • Ricky Tummon was Second Coxswain and served on the crew for twenty years from 1967 to 1987. He was on the Silver medal services to Calcutta Princess and Skopelos Sky.

Top right • Assistant Mechanic Arthur May was on the crew from 1961 to 1987 and on the boat during the three most recent silver medal services.

Middle left • Second Coxswain Edward Hicks was on the crew for twenty-nine years, from 1977 until his retirement with the replacement of the Tyne in 2006.

Middle right • John Alldridge was Mechanic from 1988 to 2003. He was Mechanic on the Secil Japan service in 1989 and is grandson of Mechanic George Pinch.

Left • Robert Norfolk was crew from June 1971 and head launcher from 1986. Peter Poole was on the crew from October 1967 and winchman from 1987.

F • Rock inshore lifeboat station

Rock lifeboat station is situated on the opposite side of the Camel Estuary to Padstow and provides inshore cover in and around the estuary. Although Rock is independent from Padstow, the two stations often work together on exercise and services. The station was established after the Padstow Harbour Commissioners approached the RNLI in 1993 and stated there was a need for an inshore lifeboat to cover the Camel Estuary and river. Harlyn private rescue service was no longer operating any boats, and incidents occurring inside the Doom Bar were being dealt with by local vessels. So in November 1993 the RNLI's Committee of Management agreed that a D class ILB station would be established at Rock, on the northern side of the river. A D class inflatable was sent on 4 March 1994 for an evaluation season.

In 1995 Rock was made permanent as an all-year-round ILB station from 8 April and the new D class inshore lifeboat D-489 *Dolly Holloway* was placed on service on 27 September, having been provided by the gift of Mr Michael Holloway. In June 1997 a new boathouse was completed, providing housing for the lifeboat and launching vehicle.

A new D class inflatable D-634 *Rusper* was placed on station on 1 February 2005 and was named and dedicated at the station on 30 April 2005. The new boat, funded through the generosity of Mrs Anita Greenwood, was handed over and named by the donor during the ceremony. The station's latest inshore lifeboat, D-772 *Rusper II*, was also provided from a donation given by Anita Greenwood, and her friend Pam Waugh, and like her predecessor was named after the donors' home village in West Sussex.

The lifeboat house at Rock was built in 1997 for the D class inflatable and Quadbike launch vehicle. It was funded through a local appeal, which raised over £150,000. The ILB is launched over the beach into the relatively sheltered waters of the Camel Estuary. (Nicholas Leach)

D-489 Dolly Holloway beign launched on exercise into the Camel Estuary in 1998. (Nicholas Leach)

At the end of her naming ceremony on 30 April 2005, D-634 Rusper is launched for a demonstration before being recovered using the station's Honda Quadbike. D-634 served the station from 2004 to 2014 and launched 189 times, rescued 135 people, and saved 18 lives during that time. (Paul Richards)

D-772 Rusper II is put through her paces at the end of her formal naming and dedication ceremony on 24 April 2015. Mike Hewitt MBE, Lifeboat Operations Manager, accepted the ILB on behalf of the station and she was named by donor Anita Greenwood. (Nicholas Leach)

The lifeboat crew 2017, left to right: Mikayla Howells, Steve Nicholas, Ian Kitto, Damion Gough, Joe Small, Michael Dennick, Michael England, Oliver Vivian, Richard Pitman, Chris Gamble, Ross McBurnie, Tom Norfolk, Steve swabey, Gary Chapman, John Dolan, Kevin Briggs. (By courtesy of Padstow RNLI)

The lifeboat crew June 2018, left to right: Kevin Briggs, Robert Norfolk, Kevin Brader, Alan Hoskin, Michael Dennick, Oli Myles, Rosie Howells, Steve Swabey, Mikayla Howells, Michael Smith, Steve Nicholas, Gary Chapman, Bryn Phillips, Ian Kitto, Michael England , Damion Gough, Thomas Norfolk and Richard Pitman. (Jeff Meachin)